BLAISE PASCAL
The Genius of His Thought

Blaise Pascal

The Genius
of His Thought

by Roger Hazelton

W

THE WESTMINSTER PRESS
PHILADELPHIA

PUBLISHED BY THE WESTMINSTER PRESS ®
PHILADELPHIA, PENNSYLVANIA

PRINTED IN THE UNITED STATES OF AMERICA

Library of Congress Cataloging in Publication Data

Hazelton, Roger, 1909–
  Blaise Pascal: the genius of his thought.

  Bibliography: p.
  1. Pascal, Blaise, 1623–1662. I. Title.
B1903.H33   194 [B]   73–21951
ISBN 0–664–20999–8

To my son
David
in loving memory

Contents

Foreword

The presence of genius in a human life always intrigues and astonishes us. It can be detected readily enough, but to describe or define it is quite a different and more difficult matter. Who does not respond admiringly to evidence of rare, unique gifts in another person, even when admiration is clouded by antagonism, envy, or despair? For genius is at once uncommon and common, a singular and private gift held in trust for all mankind. Since each of us is not simply an individual but a member of the human race as well, we may rightly regard every instance of genius as belonging to all of us.

I first made my response to the genius of Pascal many years ago, and my deepening acquaintance with his work has brought with it a profound sense of indebtedness and appreciation. This book grows out of a study and an enthusiasm that have been increasingly concerned not only with the man himself in his historical context but also with the projects and issues that engaged his attention. It is written in the conviction that to come to terms with Pascal means coming to terms with what he takes seriously, cares about, and searches for throughout his working, thinking life.

This book attempts therefore to provide a useful, reliable introduction to what may be called the genius of Pascal's thought. Considering the departmentalized character of present-day scholarship, it would require a panel of experts to account for each of the areas in which Pascal excelled and has proved influential. In his time a single man's thought could range more widely and confidently than ours through science, literature, philosophy, theology; one is reminded of Bruno and Galileo, Bacon and Descartes, as well as of Pascal. Nevertheless one must accept his limitations without becoming intimidated by them if the task of giving a coherent, comprehensive interpretation is not to be abandoned altogether.

Indeed, one reason for offering a new interpretation of Pascal is just the intolerable specialization of much recent writing on the subject. Entire works have been devoted to Pascal's family relationships, illnesses, scientific contributions, religious experiences and beliefs, political and social views, or to his predecessors and followers, his models and methods, his prejudices and failures. Psychiatrists and Marxists, astrophysicists and ecclesiastics, poets and journalists have all left their mark in Pascalian studies. But the books that try to understand the meaning and bearing of Pascal's whole thought are unfortunately few. Most of them are written in French, German, Italian, Russian, or Japanese; and the majority of those translated into English are already out of print. Those which remain accessible are generally so "scholarly" that they can only alienate the very readers whom Pascal wanted most to reach.

A second reason for a book like this may be found in Pascal's own universality of outlook and appeal. This trait in his thought is not so much due to its all-including scope as to its perceptive depth. In one place Pascal contrasts the pulling, forcing power of a hook with the attracting, unclosing power of a key; there can be little doubt that his influence has been of the latter kind. This being so, we may expect an indefinite number of reverberations and responses, each contributing hopefully to the overall picture. There will always be the chance that something has been neglected, overstressed or misinterpreted, yet each new effort at interpretation will run fresh risks in covering fresh ground.

Every interpreter of Pascalian thought looks for a thread or clue that can inform and unify his work. The best clue would be one furnished by Pascal himself, of course. The theme I have chosen here is that of man in relation to the infinite, which is rendered with many variations by Pascal. He asks, "What is a man in the infinite?" The question can be taken in a cynical or despairing sense, but Pascal's answer, "Man is not made but for infinity" makes such a sense irrelevant for his thought. As scientist, humanist, believer, artist, and philosopher Pascal is engaged in giving this answer to this question. To him, infinity and humanity are mysteriously linked and complementary to one another. That is the thesis of this book, and one that places Pascal and his thought very close to the center of our contemporary searching and striving. I am certain that we have not done with Pascal, nor he with us.

The chapters that follow are designed to convey something of the versatility and mobility of Pascal's thought, while indicating that it developed "by degrees" as he put it, and attained a genuine climax of insight and importance. The last two chapters presuppose the first four, raising issues chiefly of method and approach. My hope is that the reader will be encouraged to participate in that rendezvous and colloquy with Pascal which all interpretations must finally seek to make pertinent and possible.

It is a pleasure to acknowledge my gratitude to friends and sources of help through the years of my Pascalian studies. An appointment as Fulbright Research Professor at the University of Paris in 1951–1952 enabled me to begin work in earnest, and the following years provided opportunities through teaching, writing, and lecturing to continue it. Invitations to lecture on Pascal at Dartmouth College and at the Harvard Divinity School gave added stimulus and encouragement. I am indebted to the publishers of *The Journal of Religion, Religion in Life,* the *Andover Newton Quarterly,* and to Harper & Row, Publishers, Inc., for permission to use materials from published articles. Membership in the Société des Amis de Port-Royal has also helped to keep my interest in Pascal alive.

The impetus for this book in its present form came from an invitation to give the Lowell Lectures in Boston in the spring of 1967. To the Boston University School of Theology and to John Lowell, Trustee of the Lowell Institute, I express my gratitude. The Bibliothèque Nationale in Paris has accorded me privileges on many occasions. Conversations over the years with friends, notably the late Gabriel Marcel, Marguerite Yourcenar, Stanley R. Hopper, Charles S. Duthie, Arthur Cushman McGiffert, Jean-Claude Martin, and Jacques Massenet, have contributed much to my study. I am especially grateful to Dr. Lynda G. Christian and Professor John T. Christian for their help during my preparation of the final manuscript.

The basic source for all quotations from Pascal appearing in this book is *Pascal: Oeuvres Complètes* (Paris: Editions du Seuil, 1963). Pascal's *Pensées* pose special problems. They have been rendered into English many times; various editors have numbered and arranged them differently, resulting in considerable confusion for English readers. I have made my own translation of all passages quoted from the *Pensées* in this book. In each case, however, for the reader's convenience, I have referred in parentheses to the corresponding pages in two other published translations, thus: (E 81; P 44). "E" refers to the Everyman's Library edition (*Pensées*, ed. with an intro. and notes by Louis Lafuma, tr. by John Warrington; J. M. Dent & Sons, Ltd., 1960). "P" refers to the Penguin Classics edition (*Pensées*, tr. by A. J. Krailsheimer; Penguin Books, Ltd., 1966). I thank the publishers of these two editions for allowing me to use this mode of reference, which should assist the reader to locate particular passages within their proper contexts.

The Selected Bibliography appended to the book may be useful for following up special interests or for checking the interpretations offered here against those put forward by others.

R. H.

1. The Individual

Other nations have Shakespeare, Goethe, Dante,
Cervantes, Dostoievsky. . . . We have Pascal.
Maurice Barrès

I

Auvergne in central France is a land of opposites, both physical and human. "A cold country under a southern sky, where
you freeze on lava," it has been called. The inhabitants of
this old region have long been noted for a similar mixture
of contrasting qualities. Outward sobriety and inner intensity,
formal decorum and personal warmth, make up the human
texture of the land where Pascal's life began. One historian
of the region uses this phrase to sum up the Auvergnat character: "A combination of tartness and ardor." It is a good
clue to the personality of Pascal as well.

The chief city of Auvergne and for many centuries its provincial capital is Clermont, more recently joined to the neigh-
boring town of Montferrand. Here Peter the Hermit began
preaching the First Crusade in A.D. 1095, after Pope Urban II
made his historic speech exhorting all Christian knights to
take Jerusalem back from the infidels. Clermont has in fact
been identified with the spread of Christianity ever since the
third century, and long before then it was a center of resistance held stubbornly but unsuccessfully by the tribes of
Gaul against Julius Caesar's advancing legions.

Situated on a prominent plateau, Clermont overlooks a
plain that stretches away to the surrounding mountains, the
chain of the Puys. Because of their volcanic origin many of

these peaks are shaped like domes or cones, which gives to the horizon a jagged and bizarre appearance. Lava from these mountains was used for building the Cathedral of Notre Dame, a splendid Gothic structure of the fourteenth and fifteenth centuries.

On June 19, 1623, Blaise Pascal was born. The family lived in a high-gabled house in the rue des Gras close by the cathedral. Etienne Pascal, Blaise's father, was a prosperous magistrate with the title of king's counselor. His ancestors had been admitted to the ranks of the lesser nobility by Louis XI over a century and a half earlier. In 1624 Etienne became the president of the Cour des aides, a judicial body concerned with matters of taxation for the province. Blaise's mother, Antoinette Begon before her marriage, died when her son was but three years old; hence we can only speculate on what her influence upon him might have been.

There were two sisters, Gilberte, born in 1620, and Jacqueline, born in 1625. The older sister mothered Blaise throughout his life and wrote an admiring biography of her famous brother after his death. The younger sister had a more intimate and constant relationship with Blaise, affectionate yet often strained by competitiveness, as we shall see.

Information regarding Pascal's infancy is very meager. We do know that he was baptized eight days after his birth, as was the custom. In her biography Gilberte recalls that "he showed signs of most unusual intelligence" as soon as he could talk, "by the little answers he gave, but even more by the questions about the nature of things which astonished everybody." [1] Long afterward it was reported by Pascal's niece, Marguerite Périer, that when the boy was about one year old he fell into a kind of physical languor lasting many months, so grave that his parents feared for his life. Evidently Pascal's long hard apprenticeship to bodily suffering and mental exertion began very early—an apprenticeship that was to mark his mature life deeply.

When Blaise reached the age of seven his father decided to resign his office and move with his motherless children to

Paris. Etienne must have felt that he could better care for
his son and daughters without the burdens of his office. Leaving Clermont in November of 1631, he rented a house on the
rue de la Tisseranderie in the ancient Temple district, just on
the edge of the narrow, dirty maze of streets known as the
Marais. The family changed residences several times, moving
across the Seine to a house in what is now the rue de Condé,
then back again to more comfortable lodgings off the rue
Brisemiche near the cloister of Saint-Merri, a short walk from
where the Hôtel de Ville stands today.

In the seventeenth century Paris was a rapidly growing city
whose population almost doubled, reaching perhaps half a
million people by 1715. Although the bitter religious conflicts
of the previous century had died down when the Pascal family
arrived, the capital in Blaise's lifetime was to become the frequent scene of political upheaval and social unrest. The power
of the central monarchy was steadily on the increase, for-
warded by the astute and often ruthless statesmanship of the
two cardinals Richelieu and Mazarin. Louis XIII took up his
residence in the palace of the Louvre where he died, six months
after Richelieu, in May of 1643; and it was not until the civil
war called the Fronde was over, almost ten years later, that
Louis XIV was able to make his solemn entry into Paris when
the regency of his mother, Anne of Austria, had ended.

Etienne Pascal secured the services of an excellent house-
keeper and governess, Louise Delfault, but he undertook personally the education of his children, largely according to the
liberal theories of Montaigne. He proved to be a thorough,
zealous teacher; not even mealtimes were exempt from his instruction. Languages and mathematics were especially stressed.
His purpose, wrote Gilberte, was to encourage the natural
inquisitiveness of childhood while holding back the learning
of classical languages and geometry until a genuine appetite
for these subjects had been aroused. Her father's chief principle, she remembered, was that "the child should always be
above his work." Thus he postponed his son's exposure to
geometry until one day he found the twelve-year-old boy draw-

ing lines and circles on a tile floor and so discovering Euclid's propositions for himself. At about the same time Blaise wrote a brief essay on the pitch and duration of various sounds which he had classified and explained. One can imagine his father's pride and delight at these early efforts, which give evidence of the insatiable curiosity and need for truth, an *impérieux besoin du vrai* that would become the very signature of Pascal's working and thinking life.

Since he never had any tutor but his own father it might be supposed that young Blaise did not receive a finished or well-rounded education. That would be quite erroneous, however. Etienne Pascal's manner of teaching was flexible, but his standards were apparently rigorous. Fortunately Blaise's learning was free from the deadening effects of pedantry, rote memorizing, or the lingering scholastic formalism criticized by Montaigne. Yet it embraced the elements of a good foundation in the sciences and the humanities. Between his eighth and twelfth year the young Blaise received lessons in a wide variety of subjects and problems suited to his own aptitudes and interests. His father taught chiefly by what we would call today the project method, so that the focus of instruction was upon problems to be solved rather than on blocks of material to be assimilated and repeated.

Perhaps Etienne was anxious not to subject his son to the kind of training he had undergone in Jesuit schools, and he may have had too high an opinion of his own teaching ability. At all events he managed to give Blaise a lifelong love of learning, feeding his avid mind with the sort of knowledge that increases while it is being consumed, and encouraging skills and habits of independent investigation. What gaps there were in Blaise's education—chiefly in history, literature, and in what would be termed today the life-sciences—were simply those of the period itself, and they were significantly closed by Blaise's later education of himself which never ceased.

In Paris the Pascal family lived comfortably and pleasantly, going out often, expanding their circle of friends, and receiving invitations to gatherings of considerable social brilliance.

At first they were mostly in the company of people they had known in Auvergne but then either settled or visiting in the capital—persons such as de Mondory the famous actor and the Ribeyres from Clermont. Another family friend at this time was Etienne's former schoolmate, Jacques Le Pailleur. Apparently something of a "superannuated flirt," in Jean Mesnard's words, Le Pailleur was much sought after and moved easily in high society; he also had some reputation as a mathematician.

During 1634 and 1635 while the Pascals were living in the genteel faubourg Saint-Germain, they became well acquainted with Madame de Sainctot and her children. A celebrated, rich, and beautiful widow, she had been the mistress of the poet Voiture and kept a fashionable salon. Her brother d'Alibray, a popular poet, was especially friendly with the Pascals and introduced them to the circle of writers and *bons vivants* in which he moved. The group was much influenced by the free-thinking, skeptical spirit of the great Montaigne.

The Sainctot and Pascal children often played together, and sometimes Le Pailleur would come by to take them to a carnival or puppet show. Occasionally the two families would attend the theater, perhaps to see de Mondory play his noted role of Rodrigue in *Le Cid,* or they might be invited to a neighbor's salon to hear a harpsichord concert. After they had moved back across the river the Pascals became friendly with the high-placed family of the Duc de Roannez and his sister Charlotte who lived nearby. Then children, they grew up to be Blaise's close companions in later life. Their letters give abundant proof of their affection and concern for one another.

Young Blaise, then, was on rather intimate terms with the wealthy, privileged world of Parisian society. He must have enjoyed taking part in such a gay and fashionable scene, as he kept up some of these contacts formed in childhood for many years to come. He was undoubtedly at Court, since his father was acquainted with Richelieu's niece the Duchesse d'Aiguillon, and we know that Jacqueline was once presented to the Queen. Although he would later satirize the frivolities of these people, their light-headedness and craving for diversion, in some sense or other he remained one of them all his life.

His social opportunities were matched by equally rare occasions for intellectual stimulation outside the family circle. From time to time Blaise would be taken by his father to the weekly meetings of a newly organized club, the Académie Mersenne. The members who attended were mostly men with scientific interests like Etienne Pascal himself. The meetings of the group were lively, as members brought in reports of work in progress and propounded questions to each other in a robust give-and-take. Father Mersenne, the genial and industrious chairman, carried on a voluminous correspondence with *savants* throughout Europe. Persons distinguished for their contributions to mathematics, such as Roberval, who taught at the Collège de France, Desargues the architect, and Fermat, the lawyer from Toulouse, were frequent participants. An occasional visitor was René Descartes, then engaged in writing his *Discourse on Method* while living mostly in Holland.

Blaise was encouraged to participate in the group's discussions whenever he was present, and we may assume that he did so avidly and ably. His impressionable mind must have been greatly stimulated by these meetings, and his development as a budding scientist was accordingly hastened.

When Blaise was fifteen his father became involved in serious difficulty. He faced the threat of imprisonment because of his opposition to a change in the government's fiscal policy that had been announced not long before. Richelieu, anxious to meet the mounting expenses incurred by carrying on the Thirty Years' War, had ordered the reduction of payment of interest on bonds that had financed the building of the Hôtel de Ville. Together with other leading investors Etienne Pascal protested at this unexpected loss of income. Chancellor Séguier promptly had two of the protesting group arrested. Hoping to escape being clapped into the Bastille with the rest, Etienne Pascal determined to slip quietly out of Paris until the trouble blew over. He left his children in the care of Madame de Sainctot and Madame Delfault.

While he was away, young Jacqueline was asked by the Duchesse d'Aiguillon to appear with some other children in a play before the cardinal. Following the performance, which had charmed him, Jacqueline approached Richelieu to plead for her father. The cardinal, on being told that she was "the little Pascal," took her on his knee and kissed her, and seeing that she was in tears asked her what was the matter. Jacqueline had prepared an original poem for just this occasion which she then recited on the spot. "Bring my unhappy father back from exile," she declaimed. Much touched by her manner, Richelieu granted her request. "Write and tell your father that he can return in safety," he assured her.

So, thanks to his youngest child, Etienne Pascal came back and soon called on the cardinal at Rueil with his son and daughters as Richelieu had requested. By the end of the year he had been appointed the royal commissioner charged with assessing and collecting taxes in Normandy. He assumed his new post in January and was joined by his children within a few months' time.

II

As the family settled into a new home behind the parish church of Sainte-Croix in the city of Rouen, they found their fellow citizens in a state of great disturbance. The opening decades of the seventeenth century had been punctuated with frequent violence and bloodshed as the armed bands of the poor, whose condition was desperate, confronted the soldiers sent from Paris to keep order in the streets. The smoldering embers of rebellion had been fanned to life again in the previous summer when the Norman *parlement* refused to accept the increased tax burden levied by the king to prosecute his interminable war with Austria. Rioting, burning, looting, and killing broke out sporadically. Since the local officials could not control this new uprising, Richelieu moved quickly to crush it with his accustomed thoroughness. The royal troops were again sent in to take stern repressive action. Their presence in Rouen had created a highly explosive situation, made still worse by the outbreak of an epidemic just before the Pascals took up their residence.

The new commissioner could not have come to a more difficult or unpopular post. It was inevitable that he should become the target of intense dislike and mistrust, not only from the city's laboring poor but also from middle-class merchants and the owners of the dye factories. A pamphlet circulated in this period pictures Etienne Pascal as "watching Rouen like a vampire and constantly imposing new taxes on it." Although he worked hard to distribute the burden of added taxes fairly over the towns and parishes of upper Normandy, he was nevertheless seen by a majority of citizens as the representative of a *pouvoir central* which they had learned to fear and hate. Blaise may not himself have witnessed scenes of violence, but he was certainly aware of his father's unpopularity, and he retained a horror of civil strife and rebellion all through his life.

Local unrest and hostility did not, however, keep the Pascal family from discovering companionship—such as it was—among the government officials and lawyers who were accessible. Their tight circle provided a social life that seems to have been brisk and interesting enough, though considerably less elegant than that enjoyed in Paris. The Pascals took part in the full round of Norman religious festivals, or *pardons,* and were invited to parties at nearby chateaux. Soon they became acquainted with Pierre Corneille, trained as a lawyer and a native of Rouen but then at the height of his reputation as a dramatic poet. It was Corneille who aided and abetted Jacqueline in her poetic efforts—she won a prize for palinodes at a festival in the winter of 1640—and it seems likely that he read some scenes from his plays, or asked de Mondory to read them, at a gathering in the Pascals' salon. In June, 1641, Gilberte was married to her cousin from

Auvergne, Florin Périer, whom her father had made a member of his legal staff.

From time to time Etienne Pascal would take the coach to Paris either on official business or to attend meetings of the Académie Mersenne. Blaise accompanied his father often. He presented his first paper to the Académie when he was sixteen. It was an essay on the properties of the sections of a cone, modeled closely on similar work done by Desargues, who was much impressed by Blaise's expertise and commended his originality. Most of the other members present agreed. The one exception was Descartes, who said that he could not pretend to be interested in the work of a boy. He was however sufficiently intrigued to keep in touch with the youthful mathematician afterward, though he was his senior by twenty-seven years.

In Rouen, Blaise's education went quickly forward. Having mastered the elements of Latin and Greek grammar under his father's direction, he began to read Epictetus, Saint Augustine, and other ancient writers. He read the Bible, using the Louvain edition of 1615 but referring often to the Vulgate, a fourth-century Latin translation still in general use. As was then the fashion, he commenced the study of theology in some books of doctrine and devotion then being discussed. With his father and others, including their friend from Paris, Pierre Petit, then the superintendent of fortifications under royal appointment, Blaise continued to examine the exciting discoveries and hypotheses of *savants* such as Descartes and Galileo.

Scientific problems especially fascinated Blaise at this period in his life, but this does not mean that he neglected the claims of humane and religious truth for understanding of a more "universal" kind, as he would later call it. The milieu in which he grew up, while not discouraging totally a deepened personal faith, remained on the whole conventionally rather than fervently religious. The Pascal family seems to have been dutifully devout, performing their religious obligations conscientiously, as yet untouched by either skepticism or enthusiasm with regard to spiritual matters.

Etienne Pascal, according to Gilberte, was committed to the principle that a sharp distinction must be drawn between faith and reason, so that neither conflict nor confusion could arise. In common with the majority of his cultivated contemporaries, the son accepted this view and went on to refine it in his own later writings. Yet Blaise's mind was too acute and independent to take such an important principle simply for granted; and while it would be quite untrue to say that he ever abandoned it, he did become increasingly aware of the tension set up by these rival loyalties in his experience and reflection.

Keenly observant of what was going on around him, nimble-minded and highly critical by nature, the young Pascal did not omit the study of man from his rapidly broadening perspective. True, he was so much engrossed in science at this stage that he later blamed himself for having too much neglected human affairs; yet the circumstances of his life in Rouen would not allow him to postpone indefinitely all attention to these matters and issues. Having become acquainted at first hand with the privileged and distinguished people of his time, he was not unresponsive to the appeal of worldly grandeur. Nevertheless, he had seen enough of social turbulence and desperation to become an unsparing realist in his view of human motives and behavior. Like his renowned older contemporary Thomas Hobbes, Pascal had few if any illusions about the moral ambiguities of power or the obstacles to securing justice in the actual world. He was chary of seeking political solutions to basically human problems. Singularly unsusceptible to partisan bickering and clamoring, neither revolutionary nor reactionary, Pascal found all extremism distasteful. He tried to keep the hard middle course of sober moral judgment in assessing the human condition and its possibilities. "To leave the mean," as he wrote much later, "is to abandon humanity." (E 289; P 518.)

When he was nineteen Pascal began working on a calculat-

ing machine to aid his father in the laborious task of assessing
and collecting taxes. Through most of the next ten years he
designed and redesigned many models of the machine, running
into repeated difficulties with intractable materials and un-
trained workmen. Yet he persevered until he finally had a
model that satisfied him, and by 1645 he was offering his
machine arithmétique for sale and demonstrating it to prospective customers in Rouen and Paris. It was never a financial
success, owing to its prohibitive price, but it soon made its
inventor famous. From this time on, he was frequently referred to as *le grand* Monsieur Pascal.

In January, 1646, Etienne Pascal had the misfortune to
slip on the ice, dislocating his thigh. He was attended by two
noblemen, the Deschamps brothers, who had some skill as
bone-setters. The brothers had recently become converted to
a life of charity by a nearby parish priest, Guillebert de Rou-
ville. This priest was active in promoting a rigorous and
lofty kind of Christianity associated with the reforming movement known as Jansenism, which we shall characterize more
fully later. For three months the Deschamps brothers treated
the senior Pascal at home, taking advantage of their evangelis-
tic opportunity to convert father and children (Gilberte arrived from Clermont with her husband during this time) to
a faith as ardent as it was austere. Their own example of
frequent prayer and meditation was eagerly followed by the
family, whose members now spent much time in reading the
Bible, the writings of the church fathers, and devotional or
theological books. They were convinced, as Gilberte wrote,
that "the Christian religion obliges us to live solely for God
and to have no other object than him." [2]

Pascal's restless, searching sensibility was profoundly moved
by these visits and conversations. He was twenty-two years old;
for one so precocious, the moment of religious awakening had
been long delayed. His younger sister discovered that she had
a clear call to enter a religious vocation. They shared their
newly found assurance with each other, supported warmly
by the devout atmosphere of the home in which they lived.

This time is often termed Pascal's first conversion, this being the word then used to describe the change from lukewarm piety to deep penitence and zealous charity.

One might expect that this transformation in his family's religious outlook and practice would have lessened Pascal's investment of energy in scientific pursuits, but nothing of the sort occurred. Gilberte's assertion that "from this time he renounced every other subject of knowledge to apply himself solely to the one thing that Jesus Christ calls necessary" simply cannot stand. The Jansenist mentality certainly regarded scientific inquiry as dangerous to the search for salvation, for it seemed to foster spiritual arrogance. If Pascal agreed with this, it must have given him a bad conscience, though we have no evidence that it did. In later years he moved closer to such a view, but at this juncture his most productive scientific work lay just ahead, not to mention his deepening understanding of human nature and conduct.

At all events, his serious study of Scripture and theology went hand in hand with a series of experiments on the vacuum left by a descending column of mercury and other liquids in tubes of various kinds. These are to be described in more detail in the next chapter of this book. At first he was an interested onlooker as his father and Petit with others conducted these experiments, but by August, 1646, he himself reproduced a well-known experiment of Torricelli, the Italian physicist and follower of Galileo. As his and Torricelli's findings flatly contradicted the medieval dogma that "Nature abhors a vacuum," Pascal was soon embroiled in controversy and was supported by his father against those ecclesiastical conservatives who still subscribed to Aristotle's opinions. Already he had become involved in debate with a writer and teacher named Saint-Ange, objecting strongly to the acting archbishop of Rouen that this man's views were unorthodox and not to be countenanced. His vacuum experiments soon brought him into conflict again, this time with Père Noël, rector of a Jesuit college in Paris. He made short work of his opponent, but showed himself to be an aggressively brilliant, sarcastic

young man, sure of his facts and even surer of himself, motivated by a strong desire to excel and to be admired.

It is scarcely to be wondered at that Pascal's health deterio-
rated as a result of such heavy expenditure of himself in
different directions. He fell ill with aggravated intestinal
pain and violent headaches, responding characteristically by
forcing himself to play tennis often and by taking long horse-
back rides through the apple orchards in the Norman countryside. This went on during all the spring of 1647, but it
was of no use. His health grew so poor that by summer he
went to Paris to recover, with Jacqueline serving as his nurse
and confidante.

In the autumn, on September twenty-third, at ten thirty in
the morning, René Descartes came to visit Pascal, who was
still sick and bedridden in the house on the rue Brisemiche.
Roberval was also present, arguing heatedly with Descartes as
usual. At Descartes's request Pascal showed him the calculating
machine; Descartes admired it briefly, then went on to talk
with Pascal about the vacuum. He had heard of the Rouen
experiments but had an explanation of their results that differed from Pascal's. The young scientist and the celebrated
philosopher talked at length without reaching agreement. At
noon Descartes left, having a luncheon engagement in the
faubourg Saint-Germain, with Roberval gesticulating after him
until he got into his coach. The very next day Descartes returned alone and stayed for several hours. He gave Pascal a
careful medical examination, prescribing long periods of rest
and a soup diet. Both visits are described by Jacqueline in a
letter to her sister written shortly afterward. Although we do
not know everything that transpired, this encounter is significant as it brought together the two men between whom the
French mind is most divided, in the words of Jacques Maritain.

Pascal's first accounts of the Rouen experiments appeared
in print at about this same time, and stirred up fresh controversy among those who did not want ancient authority questioned. In November, under Pascal's careful guidance by cor-

respondence, a crucial experiment was carried on regarding the vacuum at the base and the summit of the Puy de Dôme near Clermont. It was performed by Florin Périer and some friends, and Pascal was given a full report, as the next chapter will show.

Once in the winter of 1648–1649 when he was feeling stronger, Pascal climbed the tower of Saint-Jacques in Paris to repeat the Puy de Dôme experiment. He could not have known it then, but he was to be a Parisian for the rest of his life. From the tower's height his view of the city embraced the "incomparable variety" praised by Montaigne half a century earlier. The new church of Saint-Gervais stood just below; the streets of the Marais wound north and east, bordered by the large open square of the Place Royale where public ceremonies were held. The Seine flowed slowly past the ancient, sturdy towers of Notre Dame; looking south across the river, if the day were fair, Pascal could see jagged streets leading up to the Sorbonne, its chapel lately rebuilt in baroque style by Richelieu. His view would have taken in the Luxembourg gardens in front of a magnificent palace recently erected, and the large religious establishments endowed by the royal family. Looking back to his side of the river, he would have glimpsed the formal gardens of the Tuileries adjacent to the Louvre, its battlemented tower still standing by the water's edge; the church of Saint-Roch which had just been built at the city wall; and perhaps, far away in the distant countryside, the windmills on the grassy slopes of Montmartre.

III

While Pascal worked and studied, civil war was breaking out in Paris. Since the death of Louis XIII in May, 1643, Anne of Austria had ruled as regent for the young Louis XIV and Cardinal Mazarin had succeeded Richelieu as First Minister. When the Parlement refused to register a new tax edict Mazarin retaliated by imprisoning one of its most outspoken members. This was the signal for the start of the Fronde;

barricades were thrown up in the streets; Mazarin, confronted by the threat of open revolution, left the capital and made some concessions to continuing pressure from the Parlement. Among other changes hurriedly put through, the positions of the tax commissioners were abolished. Anticipating this move, Etienne Pascal had already resigned his post in Normandy and joined his son and daughter in Paris. But they did not stay long in their new lodgings in the rue de Touraine; they left for Clermont in the spring of 1649 for an extended visit with Gilberte and her family. At this time Pascal was conducting experiments on the equilibrium of liquids, and lectured informally on the subject to Clermont audiences.

By November of the following year the father, son, and daughter had returned to Paris. Jacqueline was once more thinking seriously of entering a religious vocation, but only over the protests of her father. After some spirited clashes of will in the Pascalian manner, she got his permission to make occasional retreats at Port-Royal-des-Champs, the Jansenist convent south of Paris; but she had to promise that she would not take the veil as long as her father lived.

Her wish came true sooner than expected, for Etienne Pascal died after a brief illness on September 24, 1651. Three weeks later Blaise penned a long letter to Monsieur and Madame Périer in which he reflected on the meaning of death to a Christian and especially death's illumination of life as a "sacrifice" to God. Much of his letter sounds stiffly pious and resigned, but at one point his feelings break through and he confesses:

> It seems to me that he is still alive. . . . If I had lost him six years ago I would have been undone, and though I believe my need of him is less absolute today, I know that he would have been necessary to me ten years more, and beneficial all my life.[3]

It had indeed been an unusually close and satisfying relationship for both son and father. All three children respected and loved their father, yet it was Blaise who chiefly shared his work and interests with him. Each was free to be himself within this rare companionship, supporting or defending the other as need arose, and moving through good and bad times together. Some may feel that the father treated his son as too much an equal for his own good; but it is the note of dependence on the father that is sounded in this letter.

In January, 1652, Jacqueline began making plans in earnest to enter the convent. For the past several years she had nursed her brother in illness, helped him in his work, acted as his hostess, been his constant comrade through the daily round of life. Now he faced the prospect of being left suddenly, terribly alone. He was twenty-six, and the existence of a studious, solitary bachelor did not appeal to him. Aware that his current income was insufficient to keep up the manner of life to which he was accustomed, he left the house in the rue de Touraine and rented two floors from a banker on the rue Beaubourg. He tried of course to persuade Jacqueline to reconsider her decision, but had no success at all. She became a postulant at Port-Royal in June, and there ensued a bitter, anguished quarrel with Blaise and Gilberte over Jacqueline's share of their father's estate which she wanted to give to charity and as a "dowry" to the convent. It was, as Ernest Mortimer remarks, "one of those domestic situations in which everybody behaves naturally, nobody behaves perfectly, and each thinks the other has behaved monstrously." [4] Finally Blaise gave in, ashamed of his own intransigeance, and made over a handsome sum to Port-Royal in his sister's name.

He responded to the crisis of utter loneliness by one of his characteristic counterattacks. As his health improved temporarily he went out more and more, throwing himself into the social whirl with courtiers, men-about-town, and their ladies. He renewed his childhood friendship with the Duc de Roannez and his sister. It has been hinted that he fell in love with Charlotte de Roannez, but their letters do little to support the notion. A more plausible suggestion is that he may have contemplated an advantageous marriage for himself, to bolster his financial security, but it is hard to believe that this went much beyond the wishing stage and nothing came of it in any case.

One of the friendships formed during this so-called "worldly period" deserves special mention. It was that with the Chevalier de Méré, a man much older than Pascal who owned extensive property in Poitou and was on close terms with Parisian high society. He was the person who in company with another common friend, Damien Miton, posed the problem of probable wins and losses in a game of chance—a problem so interesting to Pascal that he worked out a calculus of probabilities with the assistance of his scientific associate Fermat.

His other frequent companion was Miton, four years Pascal's senior. He was a free-thinking, no-nonsense sort of person and well known for his cultured good taste. Described as a rather cold and enigmatic man, he was nevertheless a lavish host and an indefatigable gambler. Not only did he sponsor Pascal socially but he shared with him in conversation his unflattering view of human behavior, which Pascal found more and more persuasive and compelling.

With his friends he attended parties given in the chateaux of Poitou, where the Duc de Roannez also had a large family estate. Despite his many social involvements Pascal was busy trying to make money from his *machine à calculer,* in order to offset his mounting personal expenses, continuing to work and write in physics and mathematics, and in general polishing his image as a celebrated young genius.

But Jacqueline, from the security of her newly found vocation, disapproved of Pascal's way of life and bluntly told him so. This made him realize that he was actually in great spiritual confusion, painfully at odds with himself while struggling to keep up the pace of his worldly engagements and endeavors. The more he saw of elegant people playing or conversing with each other at gaming tables or splendid receptions, the less he liked them—and the less he liked himself. There seems to be no reason to dispute Gilberte's statement that "a great scorn of the world and a nearly unbearable distaste for worldly people" [5] came over her brother at this time. This is just the sort of abrupt reaction that might be expected; and his short published essay on "The Conversion of the Sinner" echoes this antipathy in no uncertain terms.

Pascal was not the kind of person who simply let things happen to him. Experiences such as these set up reverberations; they had to be turned over and over in his mind, and weighed for whatever worth and truth they might hold. Something in him always stood aside questioning, forming judgments, forbidding any headlong plunge or uncritical alliance. In all his other commitments a prior commitment to the truth was dominant and constant. Small wonder, then, that his exposure to the ways of the *beau monde* should have left him with some disquieting reflections about his own destiny as a man.

Nevertheless he continued and worked harder at his scientific investigations, renewing correspondence with Fermat and preparing an address which he delivered to the new Parisian Academy. In October, 1654, he moved again, this time to a small house that still stands today at 54 rue Monsieur-le-Prince, quite near the Sorbonne. Also he turned to Jacqueline for counsel in his deepening personal and spiritual difficulties. On one memorable visit he opened up his heart to her freely. This was in the autumn of 1654 when he felt most helpless, most divided against himself. At once his sister put him in touch with her own confessor, Monsieur Singlin, who advised him to spend more time in reading the Bible, meditation, and prayer. Although Pascal was not particularly impressed by Singlin's qualifications, he took this advice in dead earnest and with unforeseen results.

On the night of November 23, Pascal was alone in his bedroom reading the seventeenth chapter of the Gospel of John, the high-priestly prayer of Jesus spoken before his final suffering and sacrifice. As Pascal read and reread these words he was caught up in an experience of burning, radiant ecstasy. The vacuum in his desperate life was suddenly and mysteriously filled. From that moment onward he knew in his heart of hearts what he had to do and to become. As the ecstasy began to fade he reached for the nearest piece of paper and began to write quickly, fervently:

The year of grace, 1654
Monday, 23rd November, feast of Saint Clement,
Pope and Martyr, and of others in the martyrology
Vigil of Saint Chrysogonus, Martyr, and others,
From about half past ten until about half past twelve

FIRE

God of Abraham, God of Isaac, God of Jacob,
not of the philosophers and *savants*
Certitude. Certitude. Feeling. Joy. Peace.
God of Jesus Christ.
My God and Thy God
"Thy God shall be my God"
Forgetfulness of the world, and of everything except God
He is to be found only in the ways taught in the Gospel
Grandeur of the human soul
Righteous Father, the world hath not known Thee,
but I have known Thee
Joy, joy, joy, tears of joy
I have fallen from Him
"They have forsaken me, the fountain of living water"
My God, wilt Thou forsake me?
May I not fall from Him for ever
This is eternal life, that they might know Thee, the only
true God, and Jesus Christ whom Thou hast sent
Jesus Christ
Jesus Christ
I have fallen away; I have fled from Him,
denied Him, crucified Him
May I not fall away from Him for ever
We hold Him only by the ways taught in the Gospel
Renunciation total and sweet
Total submission to Jesus Christ and to my director
Eternally in joy for a day's exercise on earth
I will not forget Thy word. Amen.

(E 737; P 913.)

Shortly after Pascal's death eight years later, this paper and
a parchment copy he had made were discovered sewn into the
lining of his jacket. He had kept his *Mémorial* of the experience close to him during all that time. Yet he told no one,
not even his sister Jacqueline, what had transpired in his
"night of fire" lasting about two hours.

Was it only a hallucination or a genuine visitation? Probably we can do no better than take Pascal's own word for it,
since he was there and we were not. The *nuit de feu* marked
a true turning point, a definitive climax for Pascal; that much
is certain. The contents of the document he wrote will be
analyzed in a later chapter of this book. Here let it only be
said that its style conveys an immediacy, intensity, and *interior-
ity* perhaps unmatched in few writings except the Bible. The
Mémorial moves between extremes of joyous exaltation and
contrite humility, occupying all the intervening space, and
ending on a firm note of promise and resolve.

IV

Early in December, Pascal placed himself under the guidance
of Monsieur Singlin; and by January he was making the first
of several retreats at Port-Royal-des-Champs with the intention of understanding and confirming the momentous change
of direction that had been given to his life. He stayed in the
country two or three weeks, first at the chateau de Vaumurier
with the Duc de Luynes, then at the Granges, a dormitory
used by the lay *solitaires* associated with the convent for re-
treat purposes. It was during this first stay that Pascal had
his famous conversation with Monsieur de Saci regarding the
views of Epictetus and Montaigne, which was transcribed and
later published.

Pascal had known of Port-Royal ever since the time of his
religious awakening in Rouen, and he had been drawn into
some delicate negotiations with its abbess over the question
of Jacqueline's "dowry." Only after the experience recorded
in the *Mémorial*, however, did he consent to put himself under

the direct and continuing influence of the old monastery. Without that influence there would have been no *Provincial Letters* and quite possibly no *Pensées*. Or as the abbé Louis Cognet writes, without Port-Royal, Pascal would probably have been a greater mathematician than Huyghens or Fermat, perhaps even the equal of Descartes in philosophy—but then he would not have been Pascal.[6]

The story of Port-Royal in Pascal's lifetime is bound up with that of a strong-willed and deeply dedicated woman, Mère Angélique, who became its abbess as a young girl in 1602 and began rebuilding and reforming the abbey as the result of a sermon preached by a wandering Capuchin friar six years afterward. A new wall went up, the daily office was resumed, the nuns were given a more austere habit, and notice was served on the church and the world that the community meant business. Within the next two decades the reforming abbess found the marshy climate of the Chevreuse valley too humid and unhealthy and transferred her nuns to a convent in Paris for part of every year. By the time Pascal came into direct contact with Port-Royal it consisted of two establishments, with the sisters spending periods of long or short duration in both city and country. In Paris, the chapel where Pascal watched Jacqueline, then called Sister Sainte-Euphémie, at her prayers is still standing, as is the grille through which they often talked with one another.

It is Port-Royal-des-Champs, however, that today evokes the spirit of Pascal most clearly. The old abbey was destroyed by order of Louis XIV in 1711. All that is left now is the round pigeonhouse, part of the foundation of the chapel walls and pillars, and the house of the Granges on the hill above. A small museum has been built on the grounds containing memorabilia of the abbey's better days. In the museum of the palace of Versailles, too, one may see some drawings of the sisters at work and prayer, as well as portraits of the persons who made Port-Royal memorable, including one of Pascal.

From Port-Royal came the conviction that a truly Christian life is a continual striving for perfection that demands the mastery of self, a *renonciation totale et douce* of all worldly ties and ways—a search that is both spurred on and fulfilled by God's irresistible graces. Pascal found here a view of life that equaled and engaged his own strenuous, seeking nature. But what appealed even more to him was Port-Royal's keen sense that God gives what he commands, that certitude and final joy can be won according to the ways taught in the gospel. That sense indeed virtually dominated the last years of his life and brought him, some insist, very close to sanctity.

Through his Port-Royal contacts Pascal was soon drawn into a new controversy that was to become a nationwide *cause célèbre*. Antoine Arnauld, an eminent lawyer and acknowledged leader of the abbey's supporters, had published two open letters defending the orthodoxy of some propositions (said to be extracted from Cornelius Jansen's *Augustinus*) which had been condemned at Rome as heretical in 1653. He was answered by Père Annat, the King's Jesuit confessor, and the case had been taken to the faculty of theology at the Sorbonne for decision. The debates that followed dealt with two issues: that of fact—whether these propositions could actually be found in Jansen's book; and that of right—whether the statements condemned in the papal bull could be given a nonheretical interpretation. After much discussion the Sorbonne faculty decided to censure Arnauld on January 14, 1656. The faculty seemed about to do the same on the second issue when Arnauld had the idea of taking his case before the public. He knew Pascal's skill in controversy and asked him to help. "You are young, you have a fine mind," he said, "you ought to do something."

Pascal accepted Arnauld's challenge, but he must have hesitated. Was this the way God wanted him to employ his talents, and was it in keeping with his recently announced withdrawal from the world? Nevertheless his sense of fair play and his old zeal for truth won out. He collaborated closely with Arnauld himself, and with Nicole and Lemaistre, other *solitaires* and personal friends. They supplied him with ammunition in the form of quotations and suggestions; he packed his cannon and lighted the fuse. A series of no less than eighteen letters were secretly printed under several pseudonyms, appearing at irregular intervals from January, 1656, to March, 1657. He titled them "Letters Written to a Provincial by One of His Friends." Although the letters were unable to save Arnauld from the censure (and the loss of his doctorate) he had hoped to escape, they did succeed in exposing his Jesuit enemies to public ridicule and created a climate of opinion that was favorable to a more rigorous, searching kind of Christianity.

As one letter succeeded the last, usually every two or three weeks, Pascal and his collaborators worked in hiding, barely avoiding discovery and arrest once or twice. For a while Pascal did his writing at the Roi David Inn, almost in the shadow of the Jesuit college. The clandestine, anonymous nature of the whole enterprise had an excitement which Pascal must have relished greatly. His "little letters" were distributed and read widely with instant acclaim and delight, much to the embarrassment of the "grave doctors" who had voted to censure Arnauld. The author's true name was successfully concealed until 1659.

At first on the defensive, speaking up for a man who after all had been charged with condoning if not actively promoting heresy, Pascal moved to the offensive after the condemnation of Arnauld on both counts had been voted. He dared to launch an attack against the laxity of Jesuit practice and theory, especially its probabilism and mental reservations, choosing outrageous examples culled from many sources. Indeed, he gave to casuistry a bad name from which it has not recovered to this day. Obviously, he wanted to present the Jesuit enemies of Arnauld, Port-Royal, and Jansen in a *jour odieux* and selected passages from their works which tended to place them at a terrible disadvantage. But he played fair in the sense that he did not quote passages to prove the opposite of what their context had intended, nor did he select phrases in such a way that he could make them mean whatever he chose, twisting their meanings to secure a flashy but hollow victory. He was, nevertheless, a formidable opponent, the more so because of his anonymity, and an increasing number of readers were won over to the Jansenist side. In the last four letters Pascal returned to the defensive, as by that time Port-Royal was threatened by persecution from Catholic and public authorities. The carefully contrived levity, ironic naïveté, and badinage of the first letters is balanced by the dead-earnest tone of the later ones.

Without attempting here to study the *Provincial Letters* thoroughly—that will occupy us in Chapter 4—the basic conflict that occasioned them should be made clear. The Jesuits were the great modernizers and adapters of the theory and practice of the Christian life. As moral confessors and teachers, especially of those in high places, they had of course to cope with the stubborn realities of human character and conduct, without discouraging an individual's effective search for his own salvation. The manuals they wrote for the guidance of priests indicate that they looked, quite naturally, for a flexible and humane approach to problems raised in the confessional.

The Jansenist mentality and spirituality, on the other hand, was strongly convinced of man's utter depravity and helplessness to save himself apart from God's gratuitous and irresistible grace. Hence Jansenists insisted upon radical conversion and absolute contrition for one's past sins as the very condition for obeying the hard law of Jesus Christ, who commanded us to be perfect as our Father in heaven is perfect. Furthermore, the Jansenists believed that this requirement was entirely in the spirit of the gospel and especially compatible with the theology of Saint Augustine, whom they were determined to follow. Between two views of Christian morality that were so decidedly opposed there could really be no compromise.

Someone has remarked that Jansenism never learned to smile. That may well be so. There is a kind of fierce joy in Jansenism, that of the *delectatio victrix*, or triumphant rapture, which God gives to those who give everything to him; but there is no indulgent or tolerant sympathy for man's shortcomings and backslidings. Pascal, who never did anything halfway and who had found that Jansenist doctrine rang true to his own experience and self-understanding, believed that this way of putting the Catholic faith was wholly orthodox and personally convincing. Whether he could be justly called a Jansenist himself in any doctrinaire sense, he was undoubtedly at this time the Jansenists' chief champion and advocate.

Pascal's letters, furthermore, had a lasting effect upon the language and literature of modern France. Voltaire, one of Pascal's severest critics, declared almost a century later:

> The first prose work of genius was the collection of the *Provincial Letters*. Every kind of eloquence is contained in them. We must date from this work the epoch of the fixing of our language.[7]

The young scientist and recent convert, it seemed, had shaped a style worthy of the great Montaigne himself, a style formed out of many varied elements: delicious (and perhaps malicious) satire, humorous asides, pungent aphorisms, hard-hitting condemnations, dignified refutation of false charges, high seriousness of purpose, rhetorical appeals, each in its right place and brilliantly, honestly done. Writers ever since have looked to the *Provincial Letters* as models of the lively, supple, lucid style for which modern French literature is universally admired. And that is no mean, if an unintended, achievement.

V

Pascal's final years were spent in an alternating rhythm of concentrated activity and aggravated physical suffering which made sustained work virtually impossible. This last period may be the most confused and confusing of his whole career. Still only in his thirties, he looks and acts like a much older man. He perplexes his closest friends and in turn is perplexed by them. Wishing to abandon controversy altogether, he becomes involved in new and painful conflict. And yet the true character of his complex, astonishing genius comes remarkably to the fore in these few crowded years.

While Pascal was engaged in writing the early *Provinciales* in the spring of 1656, an event occurred at Port-Royal in Paris that profoundly influenced him. A relic, believed to be from the crown of thorns placed on Jesus' head before his crucifixion, was brought into the convent chapel for the veneration of the nuns and their pupils. Pascal's young niece, Marguerite Périer, who had been suffering for the past two years from a painful and disfiguring tumor near the eye, approached the reliquary in her turn. One of the sisters placed the reliquary against the girl's cheek as she prayed. Very soon the swelling went down and within a few days Marguerite had totally recovered.

The miracle of the Holy Thorn, as the cure was soon called, came to be regarded as a divine vindication of Port-Royal against its enemies in the church. It had occurred just when persecution of the convent had intensified; the *solitaires* had been ordered to disperse and even sterner measures were contemplated. The miracle of the Holy Thorn reversed this tide of fortune and Port-Royal was left in peace for the next four years. Pascal saw this event as a true sign and wonder coming directly from the hand of God. He was not alone in this, for the panel of surgeons who examined his niece after her cure also agreed that no natural or medical explanation was possible. From this time on, Pascal redoubled his efforts on behalf of the Jansenist community and gave much thought to the problem of miracle in general.

Now a new and far more ambitious project began to take shape in his mind. Encouraged by the success of his letters and by his niece's amazing cure, Pascal determined to write an Apology for the Christian Religion which would present the strongest possible case for faith to doubters, freethinkers, and lukewarm Catholics. Accordingly, during 1657 and until late winter in 1658 when he fell seriously ill again, he was feverishly putting together a large body of material—references to be looked up, paragraphs sketched out, chapter headings—with this work in view. Late in 1658 when he was able to get about once more, he discussed his plan and procedure with a small group of friends at Port-Royal-des-Champs. The meeting lasted for several hours, and a memorandum of what was said was drawn up by Filleau de la Chaise, which was included in the preface to the Port-Royal edition of the *Pensées* in 1670.

Many of his notes, at first written on large sheets with lines drawn between them, were then separated and sewed into bundles, or *liasses*. An equally large number, however, remained unclassified. These two collections of notes, some enigmatic and fragmentary, others nearly finished, make up the almost one thousand *pensées* which he left behind him. In the poignant phrase of Ronald Knox, they constitute "the ruins of a temple that was never built."

Yet although we do not have Pascal's work in the completed form he intended, we do have something incomparably better: an inward landscape opened up, "the perfect echo of our own beating hearts" as this man's lived and living reality comes into view. In a later chapter we shall mention not only the problem of the manuscript itself but that of reconstructing the original plan of the Apology, problems that have baffled and fascinated Pascalian scholars for the last one hundred and fifty years.

When he was in good health Pascal was capable of doing a prodigious amount of work. During the fall and winter of 1656 when his Apology consumed the greater part of his time and energy, he carried on a thoughtful, earnest correspondence with his friends the Duc de Roannez and his sister Charlotte. These sedate yet sympathetic letters reveal him in a light quite different from that shed by the *Provinciales*. True, a certain zeal and religious self-assurance is in evidence as he supports Mlle. de Roannez in her sense of spiritual vocation or tries to dissuade the duke from making a purely worldly marriage. The chief impression to be gained from his letters, however, is that of a warmly shared faith and devoted affection.

Pascal was also busy drafting other works which he was able to get into practically finished shape before he died.

Among them may be listed the *Writings on Grace,* for which the impetus came from the *Provincial Letters*; his *Abrégé* or short life of Christ which attempts to harmonize the differing accounts given in the four Gospels—a pioneering effort; and two pamphlets probably conceived as textbooks to be used in teaching reading and mathematics at Port-Royal, *L'Esprit Géométrique* and *L'Art de Persuader.*

Nor did Pascal's interest in geometry wane despite his other projects and his religious preoccupations. His attention was drawn to some problems connected with various curves, especially that of the area traced by a point on the circumference of a circle rolling along a straight line. He hit upon the answer unexpectedly; Gilberte says that it came to him while he was trying to distract his mind from the pain of a raging toothache. This was the germ of Pascal's significant work on problems of the cycloid, which Leibniz used later in developing the integral calculus.

The Duc de Roannez persuaded Pascal to announce a competition with a prize to be offered for solving the cycloid problems. Of course Pascal intended to keep the prize for himself and did so, publishing his results in full. This naturally angered those who had sent in entries, men of the caliber of Sir Christopher Wren, de Sluse, Lalouvère. Pascal's behavior in the affair was clearly not above reproach; on the contrary, it can only be termed regrettable. Embittered letters flew back and forth. Gilberte does not know quite how to treat the incident. Proud of her brother's achievement, she nevertheless pictures him as having abandoned mathematics long before in favor of a life of pious seclusion. Perhaps one can do no better than accept Jean Mesnard's observation that Pascal's conversion was a process in which he was always having to start over again at the beginning. Yet the publication of his *History of the Roulette* was a significant contribution to knowledge in itself.

Pascal reached his thirty-sixth birthday in 1659. He could look back with satisfaction on many accomplishments in mathematics, experimental and theoretical physics, applied mechanics and invention, pamphleteering, doctrinal controversy, literature, religious philosophy. He had worked hard and been rewarded with an eminence rarely attained by one still young. The man with the alert eyes and the proud, sensitive face, quick-tempered and high-spirited, his mind darting and penetrating in all directions, was already a celebrity in his country and abroad.

Now, however, a new kind of exploration and excellence was to be demanded of Pascal. It was the path he had chosen for himself, to be sure, but his progress was hastened by the onset of the most critical phase of illness he had ever known. No precise diagnosis of his sickness is available; from evidence that came to light at the autopsy performed after his death some doctors have deduced that he suffered from intestinal tuberculosis complicated by chronic rheumatism. Others suggest that he was the victim of cerebral cancer which brought on spells of acute paralysis. The road of spiritual progress through humility and charity was made easier, perhaps, by physical disability; or was it made harder? At all events Pascal followed his usual course in turning necessity into virtue.

He never gave in readily to illness, yet for the last three years of his life he was obliged to work at a greatly slackened pace. He could read and write only with excruciating effort and his memory repeatedly failed him. At times when he had overspent his strength he fell into a state of near exhaustion. Probably in 1660 he composed his "Prayer for the Good Use of Illness" asking God to "join your consolations with my sufferings" and to "conform my will to your own." The relief he constantly sought through diets, medicines, and prolonged periods of rest would not come. His doctors gave little help; indeed it is likely that their regimen of bleeding, purging, and starving by turns only hurried the time of his death.

Feeling that he must get out of the city, he made a long visit to the Périers in their newly acquired chateau of Bienassis near Clermont. He traveled slowly, stopping to take the waters at Bourbon. By mid-October of 1660 he was back in Paris resuming contact with his few closest friends and spending as much time as he could on his projected Apology.

In 1661 a bitter conflict broke out at Port-Royal over the question of signing a formula of nonheretical conformity. The French bishops had apparently persuaded Louis XIV that the convent, for reasons of civil tranquillity, must either be brought into line or be destroyed. In April an order was issued dispersing the pupils and forbidding the recruiting of novices; soon afterward the formulary was presented for everyone in the community to sign. The controversy that ensued had to do with whether one could sign this document with reservations or not. Pascal thought so; Sister Sainte-Euphémie thought not. The strain of conscience was severe, but finally under great pressure from Arnauld and the mother superior, she did sign. She was far from well, and her life came to an end on October 4. The cause of death was given as tuberculosis. When Pascal received the news he said, "May God give us all the grace to die so well."

A passage in Gilberte's life of her brother deserves to be quoted at length as it sums up the complex, intimate relationship between Blaise and Jacqueline:

> He could not love anyone as he loved my sister, and with good reason. He saw her often, spoke of everything to her without reserve, she satisfied his needs in every way, for there was so great a harmony between their feelings that they suited each other perfectly; and assuredly their hearts were but one heart and they found in each other consolations only understood by those who have tasted the same happiness and who know what it is to love and be loved with confidence.[8]

The statement glosses over, in Gilberte's affectionate, admiring manner, the actual tensions and rivalries which evidently marked the relationship from the beginning. Perhaps she was even a bit jealous of an intimacy she did not or could not share, and so interpreted it as being less troubled than it was. Yet when all due allowances are made, her statement seems to be essentially true. Her brother and sister were very much alike in wanting to surpass each other, in religious sensibility, in basic temperament and character. Their difficulties could only have arisen in the sort of harmony and mutuality of which Gilberte writes.

After his younger sister's death Pascal felt strengthened in his resolution to "love all things in God and for God." He became unwilling, he said, to be bound by what he considered any undue attachment or devotion toward family and friends, and he asked them to keep him at the same distance. And yet when the Périers conceived a plan to marry their fifteen-year-old daughter to a wealthy older man, Pascal wrote, rather harshly disapproving their scheme. Grief over the loss of Jacqueline may have hardened him by showing him the fragility of all human ties and affections, but he remained as much involved as ever in family situations.

In the last months of his life he sold his carriage and horses, many household furnishings, and most of his splendid collection of books. He supported the work of Saint Vincent de Paul in alleviating the plight of the poor by sharing it as completely as possible. More and more, he sought to conform his own life to the poverty of Jesus: "I love poverty because he loved it. . . . I love riches because they give me the means of helping the wretched." (E 748; P 931.) Whenever he was able he attended regular and special services at churches near his home, hobbling about on a cane.

The best remembered of all these charitable efforts was the introduction on the streets of Paris of a new system of public transportation, inaugurated with an *éclat merveilleux* on March 18, 1662. This business enterprise, which proved very profitable, was the result of conversations with the Duc de Roannez which led to the forming of a company and selling shares of stock. Pascal directed that his part of the proceeds should be distributed among the poor people of Blois, then suffering from famine, and he signed over his interest in the company to the hospitals of Paris and Clermont.

By the end of June his physical condition was growing noticeably worse. Violent stomach pains and migraine headaches confined him to his bed. His fainting spells returned. Gilberte had come with her family to a house in the faubourg Saint-Michel, where she could help her brother when he needed her most. Rather than put out of his house a sick child of the family he was then sheltering, Pascal consented to go to Gilberte's.

There he made his humble confession to Père Beurrier, priest of the parish in which they lived, and earnestly requested that he might receive the sacrament of extreme unction. He knew that death was imminent and was prepared for it. But his doctors advised against giving him the final rite, thinking it would overexcite him. A few friends came to visit him, including Arnauld who was at that moment in hiding from the police. He talked often with Père Beurrier, who later wrote down his account of the conversations with the purpose of showing how loyal and orthodox a Catholic his penitent had always been.

On the third of August, Pascal dictated his simple will in the presence of two hastily summoned witnesses, and received at last the final sacrament of his church on the seventeenth. Lingering between pain and coma, his death occurred at one o'clock in the morning of August 19, 1662. His last remembered words were those of the *Mémorial:* "May God never abandon me!" He was thirty-nine years old.

Pascal was buried in the church of Saint-Etienne-du-Mont. Today his body is interred in the same chapel that holds the remains of Jean Racine. The tablet placed there by Port-Royal pays grateful tribute to "the force and scope of his genius, and above all the admirable clearness of his mind in discerning what is false, from which it is easily seen that truth was the sole object of his spirit."

VI

What kind of person was Pascal? The French like to use the word "genius" when referring to him, as when Chateaubriand calls him *cet effrayant génie* at the end of an eloquent passage that generations of schoolchildren learned by heart.[9] But Pascal has not simply frightened his readers for the past three hundred years; he has become their contemporary and companion, calling them into a living dialogue with himself. May it be said then that what makes Pascal so exceptional is his very representativeness, his universality as man and thinker?

In Pascal's case, psychological probing is as treacherous as it is tempting, yet something needs to be ventured in this direction if his gifted and unique personality is to be evaluated at all. Recurrent illness certainly played a weighty part in shaping his manner of life and thought. Did he perhaps inherit from his mother a sickly constitution? We do not know, but bad health plagued him from infancy onward. One can imagine what it meant to be so continually aware of physical frailty, so unable to ignore it. Surely this helps to explain his abrupt moves from one project to the next, and the unfinished state of much of his work. Yet we should beware of thinking that Pascal's explorations and achievements were the result of sickness, when in fact they sprang from constant victory over sickness. Pain was an old, familiar enemy to Pascal, something to be fought and overcome whenever possible. Self-pity, a familiar trait in many chronic invalids, was not even slightly characteristic of Pascal. He took his bitter medicine uncomplainingly and courageously, to the amazed admiration of his family and friends.

What is striking, in view of his organic difficulties, is the way in which periods of painful incapacity are mingled with periods of strenuous activity throughout his short life. There must have been many days and weeks when he could only endure and wait; but energetic work would be resumed at the earliest possible opportunity. Work, indeed, was Pascal's answer to enforced passivity, which by delaying effort only spurred it on when he was again capable of making it. Against heavy odds he managed to keep his psychic equilibrium by pushing himself, against his body's weakness, into concentrated and effective activity. Of course this sent him back to bed all the sooner; but Pascal preferred the shorter rhythm into which he forced himself. He was a person who needed, and got, a large amount of "ego satisfaction"; it came, however, not from adopting attitudes of brooding or resignation but from work and its rewards.

The example of Pascal shatters once for all the stereotype of the scientist as a coolly rational, uninvolved person; on the contrary, he was passionate, impetuous, and yet objective too, as when describing his night of fire or arguing with Père Noël about the vacuum. His very curiosity was temperamental, imaginative, and so creative; the phrase "merely intellectual" is one that he would have repudiated. In a careful and persuasive study, Lucien Jerphagnon calls Pascal an *émotif avide* whom nothing left indifferent, whose sensibility was peculiarly vibrant and troubled, and who passionately identified himself with whatever aroused his sudden positive interest.[10]

Within the family group Pascal's extreme vivacity—Jacqueline wrote of his *humeur bouillante*—must have been at times hard to contend with, but it seems to have been recognized and accepted. His mother's early death removed a possible steadying influence when it would have been most helpful. Father and children tightened their circle, thus creating a hothouse environment that stimulated both tenderness and tension. The son was forced to develop rapidly in the presence of a doting but demanding father and two very different but equally supportive sisters; yet he was kept dependent on family recognition—and admiration—long after the age when children normally become independent.

Pascal expressed the same pent-up intensity in his dealings with opponents over scientific and religious issues. He could be brusque, overbearing, condescending even toward those more learned or distinguished than he (study the references to Descartes in the *Pensées*, for example). When he discovered a point of weakness in an adversary's case he worried and magnified it, sometimes to a pitch of caricature or ridicule. Yet if he did not suffer fools gladly, he seemed incapable of holding a grudge against them. Indignation or irritation were easily aroused in his wide-open emotivity, but did not rankle or fester into the future. "Always vibrating, always ready to be moved and used up, living in a rhythm that can be guessed, ever greedy and yet also generous, Pascal was made for suffering." [11]

All the same, suffering is not what Pascal is remembered for, and that is significant. He was often portrayed in the Romantic period as an individual existing in lonely, misunderstood anguish. His anguish was real enough, for he had a streak of melancholy in his nature and knew well within himself the *ennui* and *misère* he described so searchingly for others. Yet today we have to be reminded that Pascal suffered. Why is this? Because he was chiefly and by his own intention a man of action— conducting and supervising experiments, buying and selling property, managing a modest fortune, engineering new equipment, overseeing workmen, bringing words to heel in writing, bent on *changing* attitudes or situations.

Pascal's unusual facility for retaining impressions vividly, long after their original impact, led him to reexamine them and organize them into new patterns of meaning for himself and others. A sure taste for the specific fact or concrete feeling, grasped in its immediacy, never left him. "Truth held him by the heart"; he could not and would not compartmentalize himself but kept the emotive, active, and reflective phases of his whole life in a delicate and yet dependable equilibrium. He suggested once or twice that this apparent balance was maintained only by a series of quick oscillations; but the point is that he maintained it.

Evidently, then, we are in touch with a highly complex yet consistent and creative personality. The clever quip that Pascal died of old age at forty is hardly just. His body was worn out, certainly, but the same avidity and intensity meet us in the dying man as in the precocious child. His versatility was the ground of his universality as a thinking human being.

If any effort to distinguish a person's life and thought is

artificial, such a distinction is almost impossible in the case of Pascal. He would have agreed with Søren Kierkegaard that "a man's thought must be the house in which he lives, or all is mad." In placing the emphasis of this book upon Pascal's thought, we are at least assured that this is what mattered most to him.

2. The Scientist

Explorer of causes, sharp, clear, eloquent, he
represents for me the fullness of human understanding in its most definite, objective form.
                                    C. A. Sainte-Beuve

There is a sketch of Pascal in red crayon on a page torn from
a legal notebook, done by the famous jurist Jean Domat, who
was a family friend. The drawing conveys a strong impression of an adolescent youth. It shows an unusually lively and
refined face, with full lips, a large and slightly hooked nose,
high forehead, wreathed with curling hair. But what strikes
us most forcibly is the unswerving, searching gaze of the
young man's big, wide-open eyes. Even as a small boy at
home, Gilberte recalls, her brother wanted to know "the
reasons for everything." He would accept only what seemed
to him to be plainly true, "so that if no good reasons were
advanced he sought them for himself, and when he had applied himself to anything he did not give up until he found
a reason capable of satisfying him." [12]

Indeed, Pascal's early curiosity, power of concentration, and
tenacious rationality were habits that remained with him
throughout his life. Once when he was eleven years of age
he became absorbed by the fact that striking a dish with a
knife made a loud noise which stopped immediately whenever
a hand was laid on the dish. Many children must have experienced a curiosity similar to Pascal's. But he went farther,
conceiving and carrying through a number of experiments,
childish to be sure, designed to uncover the cause of this fact;
and he wrote a short essay on sounds, which was his first
scientific work. The same approach was characteristic in Pas-

cal's dealing with far more complicated scientific problems as he grew older. First, and foremost, an open-eyed and persistent realism with respect to the facts, all the facts, which had to be accounted for; then, and only then, a patient yet insistent search for the cause of what had been observed, conducted experimentally with a variety of models and under different conditions until a comprehensive principle emerged and could be clearly stated.

A considerable amount of debate has gone on regarding the place to be assigned to Pascal in the history of modern science. His "originality" is plainly a matter for discussion. Yet it cannot in fairness be denied that Pascal did much to further a truly experimental method in the sciences, following closely upon the work of men like Roger Bacon and Galileo, for example, at a time when scientific work still proceeded mainly by deduction and was based upon metaphysical assumptions either covert or asserted. This is the more surprising because even ancient science, illustrated by Aristotle, knew and used an experimental method to demonstrate the truth of a thesis that had been proposed. Nevertheless, what Bacon had called the separation between experimental observation and reasoned explanation persisted well into Pascal's own time, so that the victory of experiment over theory in modern science was long delayed.[13] Pascal did his work in the context of a scientific revolution when the ancient and medieval structures of knowledge were breaking down. Pascal's experimental realism belongs to the forefront of this revolution; yet it is by no means the mere recording of observed data but an active search for intelligibility, for what he called "the reasons for effects"—a method embracing several kinds of mental operations carefully monitored by the purpose of giving a coherent explanation.

The genius of Pascal bridged the fields of mechanical engineering, experimental physics, and mathematical demonstration, although it must be borne in mind that these had not yet become the separate disciplines they are today. Looking back over a distance of three centuries, we are also inclined to forget that there were very few professional scientists in Pascal's time—Roberval and Gassendi being conspicuous exceptions, as they earned their living by teaching—which gave what we would call an *amateur* quality to scentific work of every kind. This explains in part at least the way in which Pascal, or Descartes for that matter, moved freely from one field of inquiry into another without any sense of passing over departmental or vocational lines. The scientific and technical accomplishments of Pascal are many and diverse, significant not simply in themselves but even more in their fruitfulness for the work of those who followed him.

I

It may be difficult to see at first glance in Pascal's calculating machine a precursor of today's giant computer systems. Two models of the *machine arithmétique* are still displayed in the Conservatoire des Arts et Métiers in Paris. The machine is housed in a compact metal case about fourteen inches long, five inches wide, and three inches high. On top of the box there are dials marking multiples of ten, one hundred, and one thousand; the later model added two dials marking monetary units. Just above the dials are small apertures in which figures appear as the dials are turned. The inside of the case contains cylinders joined by rods so that they move each other whenever they are engaged by the dials outside. Thus the mechanical principle is remarkably simple: toothed wheels geared according to the numerical or the monetary system, giving readings on a drum which appear through the openings in the casing. A taxi meter or an adding machine embody the same principle.

Although the possibility of calculating large sums by machine had been conceived before Pascal, he was the first to bring it to realization. The rapid growth of astronomy and algebra in the seventeenth century, not to mention that of commercial banking and public finance, had made arithmetical calculation by hand extremely arduous. Attempts were made to simplify the process by mechanizing it, notably those by Schickard in Germany and Napier, the inventor of logarithms, in Scotland. However, it remained for Pascal to invent a machine that could actually perform the necessary operations. Pascal's *machine à calculer* could subtract as well as add, for its inventor had marked on the cylinders a second numbering which was the inverse of the first and appeared in a different window in the casing. Multiplication and division were performed by repeated addition or subtraction.

The idea first came to Pascal toward the end of 1640, but it was not until two years later that his first model was finished. It did not satisfy him so he tried again, using different materials, getting them to fit smoothly, finding workmen who could be instructed to follow his often revised drawings. The work proved so exhausting and complicated that after a third model he was about to give up, when his friends, who were amazed at his progress thus far, took steps on his behalf to secure a royal patent. This was granted by Chancellor Séguier in a *privilège extraordinaire* which forbade anyone else to copy Pascal's machine and gave him a virtual monopoly in manufacturing it. Pascal returned to his work and was able to present to the chancellor in 1645 a machine that functioned perfectly. Nevertheless he kept improving it, trying out more than fifty models in all, made of wood, ivory, leather, and ebony as well as metal. Looking back after nine years of work, when *la Pascaline* had become widely known, he could say that he had attempted a new route through a very thorny terrain and without any guide.

Pascal also took charge of an ambitious program of publicity and marketing. He prepared an advertising brochure in which he pointed out the solid, durable qualities of the machine's construction, its simplicity and speed in performing "by itself and without any mental effort the operations of every kind of arithmetic." [14] He demonstrated the calculator to admiring groups of prospective buyers in Rouen and in Paris. The poet d'Alibray was commissioned to write a sonnet on the machine:

Dear Pascal, you who understand with your subtle insight
What is most admirable in mechanics,
And whose skill gives us today
A lasting proof of your marvelous genius,

After your great intelligence, what is the point of having any?
Calculation was the act of a reasonable man,
And now your inimitable skill
Has given the power to the dullest of wits.

For this art we need neither reason nor memory,
Thanks to you, each one of us can do it without fame or pain
Because each of us owes to you the praise and the result.[15]

Other friends and associates, including Roberval, offered their
services in demonstrating and selling Pascal's machine. While
it was too expensive to be widely bought, it did attract considerable attention and acclaim for its inventor.

Finally Pascal wrote a formal letter dedicating his machine
to Queen Christina of Sweden, patron of Descartes and sponsor of scientific efforts throughout Europe. Naturally he hoped
that the queen's commendation, when secured, would greatly
increase the commercial appeal of his invention. The letter is
dated in June, 1652, at a time when Pascal was especially
short of funds for settling the matter of Jacqueline's "dowry"
and for carrying on his costly experiments regarding atmospheric pressure. It has, however, a considerable importance
in itself; for the letter introduces a distinction between two
kinds and degrees of power which are then related to each
other. After describing his machine and making the expected
gestures of courteous deference, he goes on to say:

I have a special veneration for those who have attained the highest
rank, whether in power or knowledge. If I am not mistaken, the
latter may be considered sovereigns quite as much as the former.
. . . It seems to me that the power of kings over their subjects is
but an image of the power of minds over those minds which are
inferior, over whom they exercise the right to lead by persuasion.
Among them, this is similar to the right of command in political
government. Indeed, this second empire seems to me to be of an

even more exalted order, since the mind is of a higher order than the body; and it is all the more just since it can be exercised and preserved only through merit, whereas the other may depend wholly upon birth or fortune. It must therefore be granted that each of these empires is great in itself. But, Madame, if you will permit me to say so, I would claim that the one form of power seems to me to be lacking without the other. However powerful a sovereign may be, his glory lacks something if he is without intellectual preeminence; and no matter how enlightened a subject may be, his rank is always lowered by his dependence.[16]

Pascal is not exactly modest in his mode of address to the queen. Nevertheless, manners aside, he is here expressing a view that would later become a deeply felt conviction. He held that there are different orders of greatness, not so much opposed as complementary to one another, provided that the higher form of excellence is not placed at the mercy of the lower. One wonders if Pascal had read Plato's *Republic* or Dante's treatise on monarchy, where similar problems are faced and answers are given. Behind the apparent obviousness of Pascal's statement to Queen Christina, there is the germ of a significant idea which some have called the most important in Pascalian thought, as it bears upon his understanding of man in relation to nature and to God.

"He reduced to machinery a science existing in the human mind," wrote Chateaubriand almost two centuries later. That is, he built a machine that embodied its own principles and could, as he boasted, demonstrate what it taught. Within the total context of scientific and technical advance, as René Taton has written, the *machine arithmétique* marks Pascal's original contribution in creating mechanical calculation at a decisive stage, "and opens the way to the long series of efforts leading to modern mechanical calculators and to electronic mathematical machines." [17]

Pascal was always something of an engineer who found mechanical and practical problems especially fascinating. In the year before he died he conceived a plan to have carriages circulate over fixed routes at regular intervals throughout the day, to relieve congestion on the streets of Paris. This became the first system of public transportation in Europe. The fare charged was no more than a few cents a ride. Pascal enlisted the support of the Duc de Roannez, a stock company was formed, and a royal license to operate was granted them in February, 1662. A trial run was made with a single carriage; then on March 18 seven carriages, driven by coachmen in blue cassocks, with the royal and municipal arms embroidered on the front, began moving every half hour between the Luxembourg and Porte-Sainte-Antoine. Open "to all and for all" in Pascal's words, the *carrosses à cinq sols* were an immediate and brilliant success. Gilberte herself was inconvenienced by the popular response, as she wrote in a letter to M. de Pomponne, the foreign minister:

> I waited at the Porte Saint Merry, in the Rue de la Verrerie, wanting so much to return by carriage since it is quite far from there to my brother's, but I was annoyed to see five carriages go by, all full; and during this time I overheard the blessings that were heaped on the originators of a plan so advantageous and useful to the public. . . . It is so universally applauded that you might say nothing has ever begun so promisingly.[18]

In fact, bus tickets sold in Paris contained small pictures of Pascal up to the time of the Second World War.

Further examples of Pascal's imaginative ingenuity may be quickly mentioned. There is the well at Port-Royal-des-Champs, named after him, over thirty feet deep and with a clever arrangement of pulleys, by means of which a child could draw up as much as two hundred and fifty pounds of water at a time. He perfected the barometer and the syringe, worked on pumps and clocks, made gears and winches for use in his experiments, and wore his own wristwatch which he consulted to the amazement of his friends, two centuries before such watches became common. No wonder that Pascal was called "the young Archimedes" because of his rare gift for bringing together scientific theory and practical application.

II

One of the most firmly held axioms of classical physics, buttressed by the authority of Aristotle himself, asserted that a vacuum anywhere in nature is impossible. The axiom persisted all through the Middle Ages and into the Renaissance, expressed in the rather picturesque formula: "Nature abhors a vacuum." An absolutely empty space was a contradiction in terms; since it could not be conceived it must be an illusion of the senses which ought to be removed. This was still the general opinion among seventeenth-century scientists, held on grounds that were metaphysical as much as physical. Space, whatever else it means, cannot denote sheer nothingness; hence when something suggesting the presence of a vacuum does appear in nature it must be explained as due to highly rarefied matter that eludes sense observation. On this point Descartes, with his hypothesis of "subtle spirits," was just as positive as the majority of ancient philosophers had been.[19]

At the same time, this view had been subjected to critical rethinking, largely on the basis of experiments that had been performed by various *savants* in western Europe. Galileo himself had learned from the fountaineers of Florence that their pumps could draw water only up to a certain height and no farther, yet he made no effort to ascertain a reason for the fact. His pupil Torricelli, however, did perform experiments with mercury in a tube which seemed to reopen the question of a possible vacuum in nature. This is Pascal's own description of the Torricelli experiment, news of which was soon brought to France:

> A four foot glass tube open at one end and hermetically sealed at the other, filled with mercury, then the open end covered with a finger or otherwise, the tube set in a perpendicular position with the opening stopped up, towards the bottom and plunged two or three fingers' breadth into more mercury contained in a vessel; if the opening is unstopped while remaining sunk in the mercury of the vessel, the mercury in the tube falls partway,

leaving in the top of the tube an apparently empty space, while the bottom of the same tube remains full of the same mercury, up to a certain height.[20]

Two questions were raised by this experiment: first, what was the force holding the mercury suspended in the tube; and second, what was there in this "apparently empty space" left at the top of the tube?

On the first of these problems there was a growing consensus among *savants* that the effects formerly thought to be caused by nature's horror of a vacuum could more accurately be explained by the weight of air pressing against the mercury in the basin and thus counteracting the fall of mercury in the tube. As for the second problem, it was still unanimously believed that the space at the top of the tube was filled with a material substance of some kind—air entering through pores in the glass, rarefied air, vapors given off by the descending column of mercury, or possibly a universal ether. The one thing all the *savants* insisted on was that the space was not empty. As Pascal wrote banteringly:

> All of them, conspiring to banish the vacuum, laid great stress on that power of the mind called subtlety in the schools, which when it comes to solving real difficulties offers merely vain words with no foundation.[21]

Once his interest was aroused, Pascal became convinced that Torricelli's experiment could be reproduced under a variety of different conditions which would establish the fact of a vacuum and explain it in principles that might be demonstrated and accepted without recourse to ancient dogmas. The first experiment at Rouen was made by Pierre Petit and Pascal's father, who added a layer of water above the mercury in the vessel; when the tube was raised so that its lower open end left the mercury and entered the layer of water, the mercury in the tube flowed out and the water rose to fill not only the space previously filled by the mercury but also the empty space above it. Thus it was shown that the space above the mercury in the tube, before the water rushed into it, was indeed a vacuum and not filled with some rarefied substance.

At first a spectator and recorder, Pascal very soon took charge of further experiments. Commencing in December, 1646, and continuing into the spring of 1647, he showed by a variety of methods, using not merely tubes of different shapes and sizes but also bellows, syringes, and siphons containing water, with wine and oil instead of mercury, that empty space is possible and conceivable experimentally. One noteworthy experiment was said to have been performed, in the presence of Pascal's critics, with two tubes each forty feet long fastened to a ship's mast, filled with wine and water respectively. The critics had predicted that the wine, being more volatile than water, would emit a greater amount of vapor and so would not rise as high as the water. Actually, however, the wine rose higher; the vapor hypothesis had to be abandoned, and the critics were won over. But Pascal wanted still further proof and continued his experiments. At last he was able to write proudly, in reviewing the whole series of efforts which had been costly and exhausting to his strength:

> Having demonstrated that none of the materials perceptible to our senses and our knowledge fill this empty space, until somebody shows me the existence of some matter that does fill it, it is a veritable vacuum without all matter whatsoever.[22]

Objections to the experiments and the conclusions Pascal based on them were beginning to accumulate. They ranged all the way from reassertions of Aristotle's authority in science to attacks on the originality of the Rouen investigations. One of the objectors was Père Noël, forty years Pascal's senior, the suave, distinguished rector of a Jesuit college in Paris. In October, 1647, after reading Pascal's account of the *Expériences Nouvelles,* he wrote a letter advancing again the Aristotelian dogma and denying the possibility of empty space, but without any supporting evidence or logical argumentation. Instead of proving his denial he chose to repeat the unfounded notion that "purefied air" enters through the "pores" of the glass tube. Since a vacuum was for him inconceivable philosophically, Père Noël seized upon what seemed the most likely hypothetical alternative. In the course of his overpolite and ponderous objections he gave, by way of illustration, an attempted definition of light as "a luminary motion of luminous bodies." Pascal in replying—he could not be expected to take this sort of thing lying down—made short work of this by pointing out that it included in the definition the very thing to be defined. His tone of irony only slightly concealed by courtesy suggests the style of the *Provinciales* almost a decade later. The reply to Noël is important for several reasons: it gives precise indications of the method to be followed and defines the aims of scientific research with admirable clarity. Pascal concludes by remarking that he found Père Noël's letter "no less a sign of the weakness of the opinion you hold than of the vigor of your mind." [23]

The question that was uppermost in Pascal's mind at this stage was whether the suspension of liquid in a reversed tube is caused by the so-called *horreur du vide* or simply by air pressure from outside. One way of proving that the latter and not the former was the case had apparently been suggested to him by Descartes during their long conversation while Pascal was sick in Paris. The experiment was carefully designed by Pascal and then carried out by Florin Périer in Clermont in September, 1648. Taking five of his friends as witnesses Périer went to the Franciscan garden at the lower end of the city, bringing along sixteen pounds of mercury, two large tubes, and some basins. First he repeated Torricelli's original experiment with the two tubes standing side by side; then, leaving one tube in the garden with its basin, he climbed the Puy de Dôme all the way to the summit, there performing the identical experiment again. Coming down the mountain, Périer repeated the experiment several times, observing that the lower he went the higher the mercury rose in the tube. On the following day he did the same experiment at the base and on the roof of the cathedral. Then he wrote Pascal a full account of everything he had done, including the precise observations made.

In his recital of these experiments published shortly afterward Pascal insisted that he had demonstrated, by carefully checked and repeated empirical observations of a great range of data, including the equilibrium of liquids and the operation of pumps, that atmospheric pressure is in fact the correct name for what until then had been termed the horror of a vacuum. He had not been hasty in coming to this conclusion, and had foreseen as well as answered every objection. Also he realized that there was still important work to be done, especially regarding the weight of a mass of air, for which he was already designing further experiments. In his summary of what had been accomplished he included some applications to other problems such as the determining of altitudes, the correction of thermometer readings, and the forecasting of weather.

Here is his conclusion to the review, or *récit*, of "the great experiment of the Puy de Dôme" written with a true Pascalian flourish and a final dig he could not resist at the scientific diehards:

> This experiment revealed the fact that water rises in pumps to very different heights, according to the variation of altitudes and weather, but always in proportion to the weight of the air. It perfected our knowledge of these effects and put an end to all doubt; it showed their real cause, which was not the abhorrence of a vacuum, and shed on the subject all the light that could be wished for. . . . Does nature abhor a vacuum more in the highlands than in the lowlands? In damp weather more than in fine weather? Is not its abhorrence the same on a steeple, in an attic, and in the yard?
>
> Let all the disciples of Aristotle collect the profoundest writings of their master and his commentators in order to account for these things by the abhorrence of a vacuum, if they can. If they cannot, let them learn that experiment is the true master to be followed in physics; that the experiment made on mountains has overthrown the general belief in nature's horror of a vacuum . . . and that the weight of the mass of air is the true cause of all the effects previously laid to that imaginary cause.[24]

The vivacious, lucid style is in the tradition of Galileo and Bacon; but it should be remembered that the conclusion follows a research document containing precise procedures, exact measurements, meticulously organized data, and logically ordered argument, together with fruitful suggestions for experimental and practical purposes. Thus Pascal, as Pierre Humbert writes, "completely resolves the problem, generalizes it, and adds a new and definitive chapter in the history of physics." [25]

Unfortunately Pascal was never able to finish the Treatise on the Vacuum which was to have embodied his full reflections on these physical experiments. Yet we do have a large part of his Preface, often and rightly cited as a prime example of Pascalian thought. Here, for instance, is the famous statement that "man is not made but for infinity," in which Pascal intends to emphasize the cumulative, progressive nature of scientific knowledge in contrast to the instinctual, repetitive behavior of the lower animals. And here too is the conviction that "all the generations of men, following each other in the course of so many centuries, must be regarded as one man who lives on and is constantly learning. . . . Those whom we call ancients were veritably new in all things and actually constituted the childhood of mankind." Hence Pascal would have agreed with Alfred North Whitehead that the most un-Greek thing we can do is to copy the Greeks. If the ancients had known what he knew about the existence of a vacuum, they would have drawn the same conclusions as he did. Where scientific matters are concerned, the authority of antiquity is no substitute for experimental knowledge. Pascal brings his Preface to a close with these words:

> And so without contradicting them, we may assert the contrary of what they said; and no matter what influence this antiquity has had, the truth must always prevail even though it is newly discovered. For the truth is always older than all the opinions men have held regarding it; and we should be ignoring the nature of truth if we imagined that truth began at the time when it began to be known.[26]

III

Inventor, engineer, experimental physicist—but Pascal was first and foremost a mathematician. Even if he had done nothing else, his mathematical work alone would have brought him lasting fame. Some of his published work has disappeared and other writings never reached the stage of publication, but what remains is substantial and impressive.

The story told by his older sister that he discovered Euclidean geometry all by himself at the age of twelve may be largely apocryphal. The germ of truth in the family legend may be that suggested in another contemporary account to the effect that he could read Euclid for pleasure at that age and had mastered the first six books of the *Elements* without his father's knowledge or consent. However much the facts may have been embellished by family pride later, Pascal's early introduction to geometry seems to reveal his characteristic scientific mentality—an inquisitive impatience combined with independent judgment and issuing in cogently reasoned demonstration.

At any rate, his work on the properties of conic sections is a matter of public record. He was sixteen at the time and already well acquainted with Greek geometry. Probably through the Académie Mersenne, Pascal heard of a treatise by Desargues, which he read in all likelihood with the help of Desargues himself. The important treatise set forth a number of problems posed by studying the sections of a cone, isolating three basic curves which Desargues believed could be dealt with by a single theorem. The young Pascal produced an essay of his own on the same subject, respectfully acknowledging his indebtedness to Desargues. This essay was read at a meeting of Mersenne's group in 1640. Some members urged that it be printed, and Pascal prepared a one-page summary of which two copies are still known to exist. One is kept in the Bibliothèque Nationale in Paris, the other in the Leibniz collection in Hanover, Germany.

The *Essai pour les Coniques,* as summarized by its author,

includes the demonstration of some propositions Pascal had
learned from Desargues and the Greek geometricians, plus two
lemmas of his own which Desargues himself, and later Leibniz, recognized as an original and fertile contribution to the
subject. These propositions contain what has since been
termed Pascal's theorem: If any six-sided, six-angled figure is
inscribed in any conic section, and the sides of the hexagon
thus produced are projected beyond the section, the pairs of
opposite sides will meet in three points all of which lie on a
straight line. This novel use of projection in geometry made
possible the deduction of the whole theory of conic sections.
Pascal was naturally elated over the significance of this discovery and, according to Mersenne, developed from it no less
than four hundred corollaries.

There has been considerable discussion recently about the
originality of Pascal's "mystic hexagram" and the theory based
upon it. Did he simply take Desargues's important theorem
and state it with more clarity than Desargues did, or is he to be
credited with making the crucial breakthrough into modern
projective geometry? The truth probably lies between these
differing opinions. That Pascal depended closely on the work
of Desargues and fully admitted this himself is not open to
question. Neither is it without significance that men of science
like Leibniz in the eighteenth century and Poncelet in the
nineteenth saw in Pascal's work on conic sections the turning
point which opened up projective geometry. Certainly this
possibility was envisaged by Desargues, but it was cultivated
by Pascal with such determination and precision that a new
branch of knowledge was the result.

Of all Pascal's mathematical activities perhaps the most
interesting to a nontechnical reader is his work on the calculus
of probability. It began casually, as we noted in the first chapter, with a question put to Pascal at some time between 1652
and 1654 by his friends Méré and Miton. Their query had to
do with determining chances in gambling. How many times
should two dice be thrown in order to make it worthwhile
to gamble on two sixes turning up? Pascal had no difficulty

working out an answer by simple arithmetic, taking into account the number of faces on the dice and all their possible combinations. He concluded that the odds change from unfavorable to favorable between the twenty-fourth and twenty-fifth throw.

Then Méré asked a tougher question. How should the stake money be divided fairly, that is, in relation to each player's chance of winning, if one player leaves the game before it is finished or if the game is called off after a limited number of throws? After making many calculations Pascal became intrigued by the possibility of developing a general method which could cover all such cases. He found his answer in the "arithmetical triangle."

The direction taken by his inquiry had been indicated by others long before Pascal. Figures comparable to his own were in use among the Arab mathematicians in the Middle Ages and may also be seen in European treatises of the sixteenth and seventeenth centuries. Nonetheless it is Pascal's inquiry, carried out with the active collaboration of Fermat, aided by Carcavi and Roberval, that set in motion the modern calculus of probability. Cooperation with Fermat proved especially productive, causing Pascal to observe, "I am glad to see that truth is the same in Toulouse and in Paris."

The *triangle arithmétique* is constructed in the following manner:

1	1	1	1	1	1
1	2	3	4	5	
1	3	6	10		
1	4	10			
1	5				
1					

The symmetry of the construction is immediately apparent. The vertical columns and horizontal lines of numbers are identical and can be transposed without altering the figure. What Pascal termed the base of the triangle may be formed by any one of the oblique rows joining one number in the horizontal line to the number on the same row in the vertical column. This base is capable of being expanded to infinity and the sum of the numbers in any given base is always a power of the number 2. Twenty such properties of the *triangle arithmétique* were noted by Pascal.

This figure brings together arithmetic and geometry, which the classical tradition had kept separate, in a skillful, fertile manner. What pleased Pascal even more was that he had been able to demonstrate that there could be such a thing as the mathematics of chance. His work proved that the rigor of scientific logic and the uncertainty of probability, which seem contrary to each other, can be reconciled in meaningful patterns. Without assuming that he had hit upon a method for mastering all contingencies, he realized that a clue had been found which had far-reaching consequences for calculation and prediction for many purposes. Pascal's work prepared the way for Newton's binomial theorem and Leibniz's integral calculus; it made possible the development of statistical methods constantly employed today in such different fields as genetics or life insurance.

Pascal's approach to mathematical problems was characteristically visual; wherever possible, a diagram was employed to facilitate the process of demonstration, so that evidence acquired the force of self-evidence. But this meant that calculations based on the *triangle arithmétique* remained complicated and long, whereas today they would be simplified greatly by using general formulas applied directly. In other words, Pascal was a geometrician and not an algebraist, which is perhaps why he came so close to *seeing* the binomial theorem without being able to enunciate it as Newton was to do soon afterward. An anecdote often told about him expresses this trait clearly: he was walking with some friends in the country when they came upon a flock of sheep; Pascal took one look, counted briefly on his fingers, and announced that there were four hundred sheep; his friends asked the shepherd, and learned that there were four hundred in the flock.

The last of Pascal's contributions to mathematics, and perhaps the greatest technically, was his well-known work on the cycloid—the curve described by a point on the circumference of a circle rolling without slipping along a straight line, such as a moving wheel. It is formed of a series of arches interconnected by points of retrogression. Galileo had found that the area of an arch so formed is three times that of the circle generating it; and Roberval had determined the center of gravity of the arch and of its segments. When Pascal turned his attention to this problem of the *roulette* he was therefore entering a field of interest in which many leading *savants* were participating. Whether the famous incident of the toothache may be believed or not, he began his work in earnest in 1658 after a long period of withdrawal from mathematics in favor of religious preoccupations. He made drawings of successive phases of the curve, concerned like his contemporaries to locate its center of gravity and to measure its area. As usual, he corresponded with others similarly interested.

In June, 1658, he announced, anonymously, a competition for the solution to six problems in a circular addressed to all geometricians. He gave competitors three months to forward their solutions, appointed Carcavi the chairman of a jury, and offered a first and second prize, promising that if no answers were received within the period allotted the anonymous donor would publish his own solutions. When the time had expired Pascal did indeed claim the prize for himself, under the assumed name of Amos Dettonville (an anagram of the pseudonym Louis de Montalte which he had used in the *Provincial Letters*). He would not have been Pascal if he had not been very sure he was right and others were wrong; the whole competition was a distressing affair as it shows him trying to prove his superiority in a high-handed manner that was needlessly arrogant.

After the barrage of charges and countercharges had died down, Pascal sent to the press three writings explaining why his prizes had been kept for himself. There followed some other publications in the form of letters, including those addressed to Huyghens and Carcavi. One of the letters, signed with the name of Dettonville, was later studied by Leibniz and occasioned his invention of the differential calculus. "The subtlety, ingenuity, and virtuosity displayed by Pascal in these writings is dazzling," according to the judgment of Alexandre Koyré.[27] He added his own genius to what Whitehead calls "the century of genius."

Coming as it did only a few years after Pascal's definitive conversion experience, the work on the *roulette* caused some lifted eyebrows at Port-Royal. It seemed that just when he had turned away from mathematics forever he yielded momentarily to the lure of his old first love. Was this not a regrettable lapse from that search for spiritual perfection which had been so recently begun? In her biography, Gilberte is more than a little embarrassed by trying to show that the real purpose of the work on the cycloid was to "glorify God."

From the viewpoint of the historian of science, however, what is most regretted is Pascal's flight from scientific inquiry, for which he was so brilliantly suited, into the alien realm of a "mystical" faith. What could have induced the infant prodigy to bury his talent? Thus George A. Sarton comments:

> Think of Pascal! Why do these men abandon mathematics? Is it because philosophy or religion appeals more to them, or because their mathematical work is done? They do not abandon mathematics; one might suggest, it is mathematics that abandons them.[28]

Voltaire's celebrated exclamation in the same vein was this: "There he was, sewing scraps of paper into his pocket, when it was the time to give France the glory of the calculus of infinity!" And in our own century Paul Valéry even went so far as to accuse Pascal of betraying science in the name of religion.

These quite unscientific protestations on behalf of science raise some interesting points. Why should Pascal have to be accused of "betraying" or "abandoning" anything? Such charges do not need to be refuted; but the implied criticism of Pascal's integrity both as a man of science and a man of faith should not go unexamined. Was he a person hopelessly divided against himself, torn between opposing loyalties? Obviously, this question cannot be answered apart from a comprehensive treatment of his thought as a whole, which the ensuing chapters of this book will try to give. As we shall see, the way in which Pascal shifted the objectives of his thought does not disrupt but only discloses the essential unity of that thought. One might wish, indeed, that he himself had explored more thoroughly the points of connection he intuited between the problem of mathematical infinity, for example, and the theological dimension of transcendence. In the famous and highly controversial *pensée* called "the Wager" Pascal moves abruptly from one meaning of infinity to the other; he must have felt that there is an intrinsic connection between them which, however, he does not explain.

It is different with the theme of the "Orders" which belongs to the deepest level of Pascalian thought. In the letter to Queen Christina we have already noticed this theme, expressed there with reference to the orders of political and intellectual preeminence. But the theme receives more complete treatment in a mathematical context, making its first appearance in the papers on the *triangle arithmétique* and growing in refinement and importance in the treatise on *The Summation of Numerical Powers,* written at about the same time. This treatise sets forth "a unique and general method" for finding the sums of numbers raised to the fourth power, and those of higher powers up to infinity. Methods for finding the sums of squares and cubes were used long before Pascal; he wished to do the same for the higher powers. His procedure is rather complicated, since he is still dealing arithmetically with binomials and coefficients that can be much better expressed algebraically. Toward the end of the treatise Pascal writes:

We do not increase a continuous magnitude when we add to it, in any desired number, magnitudes of an order of higher infinitude. Thus points add nothing to lines; lines add nothing to surfaces; surfaces add nothing to solids. Or, to speak of numbers as is proper in a treatise on arithmetic, roots do not count in relation to squares, squares do not count in relation to cubes, and cubes do not count in relation to squared squares; so that we may neglect as void all quantities of a lower order.[29]

No one today would find this observation particularly startling, and Pascal says it is familiar to his mathematical contemporaries. Its importance lies not in its novelty but in the way it shows "the connection, always worthy of admiration, which nature, ever mindful of unity, establishes between things apparently far removed from each other." Whether by analogy or by extrapolation Pascal adopts a similar principle in types of inquiry other than mathematics. Each order, of bodies, thoughts or what Pascal was later to call "the heart," exists in its own right and must be dealt with on its own terms; but the last of these orders is as superior to the second as the second is superior to the first.

One might draw some interesting comparisons of Pascal's orders with such twentieth-century conceptions as Karl Heim's theory of dimensions or the spheres of Teilhard de Chardin. In each of these conceptions a principle arrived at scientifically is generalized for the purpose of relating one realm of inquiry to other realms, as a reliable clue for bridging separate and very different areas by a universal, unifying idea.

IV

Interpreters of Pascalian thought often contrast it sharply with that of Descartes. The difference is spelled out by distinguishing the geometrical mind of Pascal from the algebraic mind of Descartes. Thus Alexandre Koyré writes:

For the first (the geometrician) every problem is to be solved by a construction, for the second (the algebraist), by a system of

> equations. . . . For one, a conic section is a happening in space and an equation is only an abstract and far-off representation; for the other, the essence of a curve is just the equation it suggests, and its spatial figure is only a quite secondary and even at times useless projection.[30]

Pascal's innate *géométrisme,* as contrasted with the deductive and systematic mentality of a philosopher like Descartes, characterizes all his scientific writing. As Leibniz noticed later, Pascal was one of those who saw in space a stimulus to the mathematical imagination and were therefore able to trace a multitude of lines whose spatial relationships, no matter how intricate, could be discerned without confusion. Thinkers like Descartes, however, found such efforts of the imagination tiresome and preferred the conceptual simplicity of abstract formulas. Pascal's thought, Koyré points out, is marked by the refusal of all formulas; if he did not find the binomial formula that was because he was not looking for it. His mathematical genius is expressed not in the invention of new principles so much as in the skill with which he discovered and made clear his rules or methods.

In this respect Pascal belonged to the past as much, if not more, than he belonged to the future of scientific investigation in the seventeenth century. For him there were no absolutely first principles, no pure beginnings on which a chain of reasoning can be built in order to draw out a consistent system of consequences. No, we must start *in medias res,* in the thick of facts themselves as they appear, holding practically and tentatively to those principles which at first seem solid enough, but remaining unsatisfied until patient, critical exploration yields hypotheses that progressively measure up to the realities they seek to explain.

This whole process of inquiry is one that takes place only by degrees. It includes intermittent insights, brusque leaps, crucial experiments, repeated questioning; and if it should succeed, it is solely by virtue of the clarity it brings to what was originally doubtful or obscure. Hence instead of Descartes's clear and distinct ideas Pascal proposes the use of distinguishing and clarifying ideas, which can be brought to bear not only upon science or verified knowledge but upon the whole of man's experience.[31]

Actually, what we see at work in Pascal's thinking is the geometrical mind trying to surpass itself. In one of the best known *pensées* he discriminates between two basic uses of intelligence which he calls the *esprit géométrique* and the *esprit de finesse*. These are not easy to render in English, but let them be termed the analytical and the penetrative mind. The first involves clear and consistent thinking from a few principles of which most people are not normally aware. The second involves thinking on the basis of many maxims known to everybody, but which are so numerous and conflicting that they tend to cancel each other out, yielding only confusion and error in the long run. ("He who hesitates is lost" keeps strange company in common sense with "Let tomorrow take care of itself.") Pascal would like to reach a fineness of perception in the second realm which can match the distinguishing clarity achieved in the first; but he realizes that this is a different kind of enterprise requiring different methods.

While he is not about to give the prize to one over the other, Pascal's own sympathies in his later years appear to be more and more with the *esprit de finesse*, since he has himself felt the crudity and sterility of analytical constructions where human values are concerned. Not that he is ready to abandon utterly the search for viable, illuminating principles regarding man; just the opposite. He does not say "Damn consistency!" with Emerson. Yet he has discovered for himself that in characteristically human situations, unlike mathematical and physical problems, one must "see the thing all at once with a single glance, and not by rational progression, at least to a certain degree." And this is also why he judges Descartes to be an unreliable guide in human affairs; for as Brunschvicg wrote, if Descartes is the man of one method, applicable to everything everywhere and always, Pascal is the man of many methods, each appropriate and dependable with reference to whatever is before it.[32]

In the summer of 1660, only two years before he died, Pascal was staying with the Périers at their chateau near Clermont. He was then in great physical pain; he had come down from Paris, traveling mainly on canal boats, and was evidently much occupied with his Apology. During the visit with his sister's family he received a cordial letter from Pierre de Fermat in which the lawyer-mathematician of Toulouse suggested that they meet at some convenient midway spot for a conversation on problems of mutual interest. Pascal replied:

> Monsieur, you are the most gallant man in the world and I am certainly among those who can best appreciate your qualities and admire them unboundedly. . . . I must also tell you that although I regard you as the greatest mathematician in Europe that is not the quality which would have attracted me; but I found so much wit and honesty in your conversation that I sought you out for this reason. For, to speak frankly, I consider geometry the highest form of mental exercise, but at the same time I know it to be so useless that I find little difference between a man who is only a geometrician and a skilled workman. So I call it the finest trade in the world, and I have frequently said that it is excellent for testing one's faculties, but not for the exertion of one's full powers, so that I would not take two steps for geometry, and I am sure you hold the same opinion as I do.[33]

That sounds like Pascal's farewell to mathematics and as such it was probably intended. The important thing to be learned from the letter, however, is that Pascal only withdrew from scientific work when he had satisfied himself that he knew personally what it was about and could attain. His change of attitude was rooted in a deepening conviction that, as one of the *pensées* has it, the truths of mathematics do not console us in a time of affliction. Truths of another and Pascal would say a higher order are needed for that.

Therefore it is both unfair and unwise to try to set in opposition the *savant* and the *croyant*, the man of science and the man of faith, in Pascal. It is much more interesting and instructive to see how these two made one whole man, reinforcing each other in a quite remarkable way. This will be one of our major aims in the chapters that follow.

3. The Humanist

Pascal possesses, in the highest and most
intense degree, the sense of what it means
to be a human person.

C. A. Sainte-Beuve

Today in every center of learning a debate is going on between the scientists and the humanists. It may take shape
around any one of several issues—the relative place of facts
and values in education, the rights of persons against the en-
croachments of technology, or concern over the supposed
moral neutrality of science. This debate was not unknown to
Blaise Pascal, although it assumed a different form in his
century than it does in ours. One of the *pensées* allows us to
overhear his interior dialogue:

> I had spent a long time in studying the abstract sciences, and
> I was much discouraged at how little communication I could have
> with others on these subjects. When I began to study man, I
> realized that these abstract sciences were not his distinctive
> realm, and that I was getting further away from my own con-
> dition in pursuing them than others were in ignoring them. I
> excused others for knowing so little, but at least I thought I would
> find plenty of companions in the study of man. . . . I was wrong.
> There are even fewer who study man than those who study
> geometry. (E 756; P 687.)

Asking himself why this was so, Pascal ventured the opinion
that perhaps it is better for man, if he wants to be happy,
not to know too much about himself. But he could scarcely
be expected to rest in that conclusion; what he really believed
was that the proper study of mankind is man, however it may
threaten human composure and complacency.

When he turned to the study of man after spending a major part of his life pursuing other kinds of knowledge, Pascal saw quickly that he could not proceed by means of scientific demonstration. No abstract analysis can possibly account for the complexity and individuality of the human subject. What is needed, he decided, is a whole battery of methods at once flexible enough to reach the truth about man yet also reliable enough to elicit and confirm our understanding of ourselves. Man, whatever else he may be, is not an abstract noun. His heart has its reasons which reason cannot know. The proper study of man, therefore, is self-knowledge capable of penetrating the reasons of the heart.

This might seem to put Pascal on the side of the humanists against the scientists; but that impression would be far too simple and misleading. He brought with him into his study of man the same respect for facts, the same need of truth, which had motivated his mathematical inquiries. His change of front, if it can be called that, involved no abandonment of critical judgment and reasoned argument; and it brought into play everything that had been learned in the school of science. Yet Pascal saw and wanted others to see that human being cannot be reduced by analysis or abstraction to any other kind of being. He may have posed too sharply for our present taste the contrast between scientific and humane study. He was, however, a man of the Renaissance and shared in the preoccupation of his time with what makes men and women uniquely human in relation to the new conception of the physcial universe which threatened to supplant the Biblical-Christian understanding. Geometry would have been easier and safer for him, but he preferred to get on with the hard job of making man comprehensible to himself.

I

The book known as the *Pensées* contains many things, but the thrust of its approach as well as the source of its enduring appeal lies in Pascal's portrayal of what being human means.

It is in part a self-portrait, as any essay in human understanding must always be; but just because it is this, it is also more—a mirror capable of reflecting the human qualities of successive generations and diverse cultures to themselves. An honest individuality is always the best guarantee of a convincing universality. It should also be remembered that in Pascal's time it was still possible to think of man—that is, what makes any man or woman fully and truly human—as a certain magnitude of creation viewed in cosmic perspective. Where Pascal writes "man" we should read "Everyman" in the sense of the classical Christian tradition; yet we should also be aware that the typically modern ills of doubt and self-estrangement were already present, bringing with them those symptoms of anxiety, nausea, or nothingness which Pascal knew quite as well as Heidegger or Sartre in our own century.

Scientist that he is, Pascal proposes to show man to himself by asking the question of his place within the order of nature. Like many of his contemporaries in France and elsewhere, he is responding to the challenge offered by new geographical and astronomical discoveries, especially to their effects upon human consciousness and sensibility. Perspectives have been opened up that stagger the imagination, upset tradition, and fascinate intelligence. It is in such an unsettled and unsettling period that Pascal's restless but determined search for truth proceeds in a spirit curious yet anxious, "torn between the contrary emotions of admiration and apprehension . . . in a world of shifting values." [34]

In relation to nature, man is a middle-sized fact, suspended between two infinities and marked by a strange disproportion. He is *ni ange ni bête,* neither angel nor animal, yet he looks in both directions and shares both natures. Therefore he is a question to himself; his very existence, as Saint Augustine had declared more than a thousand years earlier, is bent into the shape of an interrogation point. Pascal writes:

> So let man contemplate the whole of nature in her full and
> splendid majesty and turn his attention from the low things that
> surround him. Let him gaze on that brilliant light, set like an

eternal lamp to light up the universe; let the earth seem but a point in terms of the vast revolution which that star goes through, and let him be amazed that this great revolution is itself a mere point in comparison with the revolution of the stars in the encompassing firmament. . . . The whole visible universe is but a speck in the ample bosom of Nature. . . . Nature is an infinite sphere, the center of which is everywhere, the circumference nowhere.

Returning to himself, from his remote little corner where he is lodged—I mean the universe—let man estimate at their real value his kingdoms, cities, himself. *Qu'est-ce qu'un homme dans l'infini?* (What is a man in the infinite?)

After a further paragraph on the infinity disclosed in the smallest possible object, opening up "a new abyss," Pascal continues:

For what is man in nature? A nothing, compared with the Infinite; an all, compared with the nothing; a mean between nothing and everything. . . . He is equally unable to see the Nothing from which he came and the Infinite in which he is included. . . .

So let us take our measure. We are something, not everything. . . . Extremes elude us. . . . Nothing stays for us. . . . Man, for instance, is related to all that he knows. His existence requires space, time, movement, elements to compose him, warmth and food to nourish him, air to breathe. . . . He is in a dependent relationship to everything. . . . Man is to himself the most amazing thing in nature. . . . This is the height of his problem and yet it is his very being. (E 390; P 199.)

Viewed in this cosmic frame, man is indeed his own kind of being quite unlike any other, and it is well that he should be impressed by his uniqueness in the scheme of things entire. But he seems woefully out of scale, a finite being caught between two encroaching infinities either of which opens out upon an abyss—a real void of both matter and spirit. It is because of our disproportion that we lack a true perspective, which is only possible from a definite standpoint: "Nothing stays for us." This is pictured in a series of evocations like the following:

> We are sailing over a vast milieu, always unsure and afloat, pushed from one extremity to the other; whatever fixed point we try to tie to and make fast, it gives way and leaves us, and if we follow it, it eludes our grasp, slips away from us and avoids us with an eternal avoidance. (E 390; P 199.)

Although he did not accept the Copernican conception of the physical universe as established scientific truth, despite its growing endorsement among his contemporaries, Pascal certainly seems to have gotten its essential message. His own view has more affinity with Giordano Bruno's: an open universe stretching to infinity and deprived of its geometrical center, in which nothing is naturally stable or secure. Like Francis Bacon, Pascal believed that man and the universe are incommensurable, and that therefore we should not suppose what is actually fluctuating to be fixed.

How is man to take his measure when the very means of measurement are denied him? Just as aboard ship, when everything is in motion equally, nothing seems to move at all. We yearn for a standing ground capable of providing a dependable viewpoint, but in Pascal's words the foundation cracks and the earth opens up into new abysses on every hand. A slippery relativism, forced upon us by a hard look at the scientific universe, gives neither a purchase nor a perspective on reality. The comforts of a benign cosmos favorable to human growth and knowledge are likewise forbidden us. "How many realms there are which know us not!" (E 79; P 42.)

This, says Pascal, is our veritable situation, and he sketches it in language of compelling force. Pascal's interpretation of man's place in the universe is not a novel one; there are distinct reverberations of Rabelais and Montaigne, and even more important, of Nicholas of Cusa and Giordano Bruno. But the resonance set up by the portrayal of a universe without center or circumference, and hence silent rather than signifying God, is Pascal's own. *"Le silence éternel de ces espaces infinis m'effraie"* ("The everlasting silence of these infinite spaces frightens me"). (E 392; P 201.) Recent efforts to interpret this anguished cry as that of the atheist or free-thinker whom Pascal is trying to convert, rather than Pascal's own confession, have not succeeded in their aim. The silence of the physical universe as newly revealed by science is a datum for the believer and the nonbeliever alike. If man would find intelligibility and purpose for his life, he must look elsewhere. This is surely Pascal's view.[35]

The disproportion of man signifies for Pascal not only anguish and uncertainty but also paradox and self-contradiction. Can a part of the picture *see* the picture? The senses, for example, have so limited and confusing a range that they cannot accurately register extremes of heat and cold, sound and silence, light and darkness. Far from being the model for all knowledge, as some philosophers after Pascal had the temerity to assume, sensation demonstrates the paradox at the heart of all attempts to know what reality is like. Indeed, our knowledge is a form of ignorance because it is knowing that we do not know. The converse of this proposition is equally important, however: our ignorance is also a form of knowledge, or more properly, self-knowledge. It is needful, Pascal thinks, for man to be instructed as to the depth and extent of ignorance in finite experience.

Finitude—this is the undeniable signature of everything human. To exist at all is to be bounded, limited, actually "on edge"; and that is both a general, objective truth about man and a description of man's inner state. Almost certainly, Pascal would have approved Paul Tillich's definition of anxiety as "finitude, considered as my own finitude." Because man knows himself to be finite he is anxious. That is his natural condition. It could hardly be otherwise, when man is suspended, dangling in infinity, which may become in turn an experience of being stifled and confined by infinity.

In a perspective that is determinedly scientific, infinity can have no place except as a kind of vanishing point. Yet man must cope with it and try to comprehend it, whether he calls it God or nothing. Is man not made for infinity, despite being out of all proportion to it? Can his mind, then, possibly come to rest in anything else?

Although Pascal could demonstrate that nature has no horror of a vacuum, he had no such answer ready in the case of man. There is a story that in his last years when he was very ill Pascal would sometimes feel himself to be on the brink of an *abîme*, or abyss, which appeared without warning on his left side, so that he was constrained to walk about his room while holding onto a chair. He did not refer to this experience directly himself, and his biographers do not regard it as authentic, although it has become part of the Pascalian legend. But whether the story is true or not, Pascal did become aware of an emptiness crouching at the core of human nature itself —a menacing, invading nothingness that is present to man as a kind of insidious absence. By now, of course, themes such as this are familiar in the writings of existentialists. Yet they are sounded by Pascal at the height of the Renaissance as confidence in human reason and progress was approaching its peak. One of the most remarkable features of Pascal's portrayal of man is that it is both modern and postmodern at the same time.

Almost two centuries before Søren Kierkegaard, during the first triumphs of modern science, Pascal asked the existential question about man:

> When I consider the short span of my life, swallowed up in eternity before and after, "the memory of a passing guest lodged for a day," the little space which I fill and even see engulfed in the infinite immensity of spaces which I do not know and which do not know me, I am afraid and astounded to find myself here instead of there, for there is no reason at all why here instead of there, why now instead of then. Who has put me here? By whose order and direction have this place and time been assigned to me? (E 116; P 68.)

While Pascal is neither the first nor the last to ask such questions, his way of posing them is singularly forceful and magnetic, as successive generations of readers have discovered. Introspective inwardness and resolute objectivity rarely occur together as they do in Pascal's thought. Even on the physical plane of his existence, man is the being who questions his location and duration in the whole of things. Moreover, he is not simply a question to himself, but must also call in question the very possibility of any answer that is presumed to come to him from the real world.

II

On the moral plane where purpose, choice, and action are concerned, man is still more miserable. The physical universe may crush him, yet he is superior in knowing what the universe does not know, namely, that he is at its mercy. But what sort of advantage is that? His condition is one of restlessness, inconstancy, unbearable ennui. He is in ceaseless motion, as aboard ship, but this may well be only another name for inertia. He has neither stars nor compass to keep him on his course. His judgments of value are not to be trusted since they are always more or less the projections of his feelings, which are notoriously inexact and misleading. He is a creature of sheer circumstance; trivial or accidental happenings like the buzzing of a fly, standing too close or too far away, taking too much wine (or too little!) control one's use of his mind and will, when it ought to be the other way around. And quite apart from built-in liabilities of this kind, man is forever being thrown off his guard by taking appearances as if they were realities. He is in bondage to what Pascal, strongly influenced by Montaigne, calls the *puissances trompeuses,* deceiving powers: imagination, custom, and self-love.

Imagination is "that dominant part of man, mistress of error and falsehood, and all the more deceitful because it is not always so, as it could be an infallible rule of truth if only it were always lying." Pascal's treatment of the subject, generally ironical, includes examples such as these:

> Suppose the greatest philosopher in the world on a plank wider than necessary for his safety, but hanging over a precipice; though his reason convinces him of its strength, his imagination will win out. Most people cannot bear the thought without growing pale and breaking into a sweat. . . . We cannot even look at a lawyer

in his cap and gown without forming a favorable opinion of his competence. . . . Love or hate alter the face of justice; and how a lawyer who is well paid in advance finds the case he pleads to be more just! . . . If doctors possessed the real art of healing, they would not need to wear square caps. . . . Having merely imaginary knowledge, they must dredge up these empty emblems by which they gain respect. (E 81; P 44.)

Rather often Pascal seems to mean by "imagination" what Socrates in the Platonic dialogues meant by "opinion"—guesswork without evidence or reason:

I would very much like to see an Italian book which I know only by its title, which alone is worth the price of many books— *dell' opinione regina del mondo* (concerning opinion, queen of the world). I subscribe to it without knowing it, except to what if anything is false in it. (E 81; P 44.)

The point of these illustrations and observations is plain enough. More tersely than Montaigne and less abstractly than Descartes, Pascal is saying that the balance of human reason, precarious in any case, is easily upset by the imagination. This is all the more unfortunate since it affects the practical business of living to such a great extent. He goes on:

Children who frighten themselves by blackening their faces. They are only children, but what is weak in childhood gets strong with advancing age. We only change our fancies. All that is made perfect by progress also perishes by progress. All that has been weak cannot become absolutely strong. It is all very well to say, "He has grown up, he has changed"; he is also the same. (E 153; P 779.)

The other instances Pascal gives, culled from his reading and his own experience, such as the magistrates robed like furry cats or the Grand Sultan (a very ordinary man) in his magnificent seraglio surrounded by forty thousand janissaries, point up the moral he is driving at: imagination seems to have been given us for the express purpose of leading us into inevitable error. Whether it takes the form of sudden fancy magnifying incongruities or oddities, pretentiousness disguised as expertise, or opinion as a shoddy substitute for knowledge, imagination is a chief source of human *misère*.

It is just a bit astonishing that Pascal should never have a good word to say for the imagination. Like Saint Theresa, he thinks of it as "the fool in the house," something to be bridled and reined in, not trusted and encouraged. Indeed, the very imaginative character of his own description of the *puissance trompeuse* which he is noticing seems to have escaped him altogether. Is this blind spot due to his essential sobriety, the love of plain statement which he shared with most of those who formed the taste of his age? Or is it due to his early training and experience in using rigorously scientific methods? It is possible, too, that even when disparaging imagination, Pascal knows that he must make concessions to it. Whatever the reason, he is suspicious of any substitution of image for reality, as his comments on the theater and painting indicate. Yet his own brilliant imaginative achievements, illustrated by the dramatic flair in the *Provincial Letters* and the gift for human portraiture in the *Pensées,* mitigate considerably the harshness of his judgments. Pascal is typical of his time in identifying the image-making faculty with fancy or fantasy, regarding it as grossly inferior to "judgment"; one looks almost in vain within the seventeenth century for any thing comparable to Wordsworth's later distinction between the imaginative and the imaginary.

The second of the deceiving powers is *coutume* or *habitude*. Custom for Pascal signifies the human inertia that prefers repetition to honest reflection, takes what is merely accidental or relative as having legitimate authority, and settles back into the *status quo* without so much as questioning the right of the past to rule the present and the future. It is custom that keeps ancient prejudice alive long after it has ceased to be pertinent or even plausible; and it is custom too, paradoxically, that quickly fashions overnight traditions which can claim to be usual and habitual tomorrow. What imagination invents, custom maintains in force. Bacon's Idols of the Cave and the Tribe have their counterpart in Pascal, who

writes: "Custom is our nature. . . . Custom is a second nature. . . . What is nature? Is not custom natural? I greatly
fear that nature itself is only our first custom, as custom is
second nature." (E 194, 241; P 419, 126.)

Whether he borrowed this use of "second nature" from
Aristotle or not—it can be found also in the *Nicomachean
Ethics*—Pascal is here anticipating, in a highly suggestive
manner, the much later view of so-called "laws of nature" as
pragmatic generalizations based on regularity and repeata-
bility of behavior. According to the pragmatic interpretation,
the word "law" is used in science only for descriptive and
predictive purposes; it should not be confused with its meaning in society, as prescriptive, binding regulation of human
conduct, enforced by penalties and sanctions.

Our impression that nature is "law-abiding" is due in large
part to the strength of custom, which sees recurrence and repetition everywhere it looks. But custom by itself cannot validate
this impression; that is the prerogative of observation and
reason. Yet even here custom plays a pervasive role: "Nature
imitates herself. . . . Nature always begins the same thing
again, years, days, and hours; spaces in the same way, and
numbers, follow closely upon each other and so a kind of infinity and eternity is formed." (E 954, 347; P 698, 663.) Who
knows then but what nature's "laws" may be no more than
man's habitual responses projected outward on the facts
themselves? At any rate, Pascal does not give a simple Yes or
No in answer to the question which was at issue between Socrates and the Sophists, whether the way things are is only the
way they seem. If nature is only our custom, perhaps this is connected in some dark and desperate way with the original fall
of man, when he broke his essential contact with truth coming from the real. Pascal's thought contains more than a
soupçon of the belief that such may be the case.

However, it is with reference to social and political affairs
that the force of custom becomes most evident. Consider this
pensée, as concise as it is famous: "Cleopatra's nose—if it had
been shorter, the entire face of the earth would have been

changed." (E 90; P 413.) Why should the political fortunes of
mankind have to depend upon the fact that the queen of
Egypt had a pretty face? Only because of the insidious influence of custom which regards governments as instituted
and upheld by God himself, when they are really established
by coalitions, war, or accidents that might have been quite
different. Thus chance, under the inveterate working of custom, takes on the appearance of cause and effect. It is out of
such fragile stuff as this that the rise and fall of empires, and
indeed the whole web of history, is woven.

It is not surprising that Pascal should often have been
taken to task for treating serious matters far too lightly and
so disparaging the worth of social or political idealism. More
than once he has been gravely charged with being a pessimist
or a reactionary. Did he, as Jacques Maritain has asserted,
want men to believe in justice without believing in it himself? Or was his "Christian cynicism," hardened in the school
of Jansenism, the unconscious preparation for French despot
ism in the eighteenth century? These suspicions have sometimes been voiced to bring Pascal into discredit as a social
thinker. Can any reply be made on his behalf to such criticisms?

It must be granted that Pascal's thought regarding human
society, unlike his view of human individuality, is lacking
in profundity. His categories are too few and narrow to
probe the depths of social experience, and his mind seems
to be made up in advance on many of the most important
issues. When this has been admitted, however, it may still be
argued that he remains a significant if not creative social
thinker. His view accords with that of Plato's *Republic* in
emphasizing the part played by illusion in keeping peace
and order within the state. Philosophers may know better, but
the common man does not and should not be disabused of
his "necessary fictions" and customary error. "All our established laws will be considered just without being examined,
merely because they are established." (E 198; P 645.) One may
easily find parallels in Hobbes's *Leviathan* or Machiavelli's

The Prince. And with a look toward the future, very similar views occur in the writings of Jean-Jacques Rousseau, who agrees that regardless of what we may prefer to think, might makes right in actual politics and it is convention or contract based on pooled self-interest that makes government possible in the first place. One may also see this same motif at work in the comprehensive, fair-minded philosophy of law put forward by Montesquieu in the eighteenth century. He was definitely influenced by Pascal, and his sharp criticism of the Bourbon monarchy was instrumental in bringing about the French Revolution.

Pascal's social thinking, in the sketchy form in which we have it, is neither eccentric nor extremist. Furthermore, it is a deliberate departure from medieval theories of society. Saint Thomas Aquinas had held that human laws are binding and authoritative by virtue of their derivation from the natural law, which in turn reflects the eternal law of God. Hence, in order for any law to be just it should meet the conditions laid down by nature for human survival and fulfillment. To Thomas it seemed a plain, unquestionable truth that human laws can meet these conditions and so fulfill the law of God for man. But this is not so for Pascal, who had seen too much oppression and revolt in his time ever to be a medievalist in political theory. He knew too well how laws are made, and broken, to accept divine authority as their explanation or justification.

Then, too, Pascal has Christian reasons for his so-called cynicism. Does not man's acceptance of conventional illusion for the sake of keeping the peace befit his sinful creatureliness? Whatever may have been true of Adam and Eve in Eden when God came to call in the cool of the evening, things are different now. The illusion that a law is just merely because it is a law must be regarded as yet another sign of man's fall from a state of grace and truth. Customary self-deception hardened into social convention is simply a fact of human existence; and Pascal calls attention to it not to praise it but to make it aware of itself so that it may be overcome.

The third of the *puissances trompeuses* is self-love or *vanité*, which is the most sly and underhanded of all. Pascal employs this word in its double meaning of self-centeredness and vacuity or hollowness. What he intends to say is that when one's self fills *all* the space of his interest and effort, then there is nothing left at the *center* of one's life. Indeed, there is no center, for the center has become the circumference. Therefore self-love, when examined candidly and personally, reveals a new abyss, an aching void in man's most inward sense of his existence. Pascal believed firmly that selfhood, taken absolutely, is an absolute zero.

The most familiar of his *pensées* on this subject is the following:

> Vanity is so anchored in the heart of man that a soldier, a roustabout, a cook, a porter, brags and likes to have admirers. Even philosophers want this. And those who write against vanity want to have the glory of having written well; and those who read want the glory of having read them; and I who write this have this wish, perhaps, and possibly those who read it . . . (E 94; P 627.)

Notice how Pascal's thought, starting with a general proposition, is not content merely to particularize it, but moves deftly in upon the person to whom the proposition is addressed. "Wounding from behind" was Kierkegaard's way of putting this form of an argument *ad hominem* in which the burden of proof is shifted from author to reader in a quite remarkable *tour de force*. Here the truth of Pascal's proposition is not to be decided by giving a questionnaire or psychological test to a fair sampling of mankind; it depends upon his singling out the reader for a private talk with himself about himself. Pascal's writing on "man" have this quality of *existential* communication to a very rare degree, which is why they have such lasting freshness, poignancy, and surprise in them.

In one sense, this *pensée* may be taken as Pascal's confession that vanity cannot be eradicated merely by being exposed in discussion; but in another sense, quite as emphatic as the first, it simply reinforces the proposition by personalizing it. Indeed, Pascal leaves it wholly up to his reader whether the attribution of *vanité* to him is fair or not. His theory of man may be shattered if the charge is denied honestly, but that is a chance Pascal is more than willing to take. At all events, Pascal's own understanding of himself seems to justify it, and what he has seen of other human beings tends to confirm him in his judgment.

But Pascal goes even further. The *pensée* that has caused more contention than any other over his view of man is probably this one:

> *Le moi est haïssable* (The ego is hateful). . . . In a word, the ego has two qualities. It is unjust because it makes itself the center of everything. It is unfair to others in wanting to be served by them, as each *moi* is the enemy and would like to be the tyrant of all the others. (E 141; P 597.)

Voltaire, as might be expected, was among the first to take Pascal to task for his portrait of man as wicked and wretched at the heart of his being. It is not right, he says, to impute to the essence of human nature an unlovely trait that belongs only to some people; one must therefore take the side of "humanity" against Pascal (*Lettres Philosophiques*, No. 25). Another fairly typical objection is that of Jacques Rennes, who thinks that Pascal's most serious fault is to be found in his polemic against self-love, since it expresses a disdain and even a contempt for "natural" man.[36]

Does Pascal analyze human motivation much too harshly in a way that must be regarded as "against man"? Pascal has left it to the individual reader to decide. But consider this observation:

> Each man is a whole to himself; for him when dead, everything else is dead. From which it comes about that each man thinks he is everything to everyone else. (E 164; P 668.)

Is it not certainly true that when I die, my world dies with me? Insofar as my experience has reflected the real world, responded to it, and added to it, that world—or portion of the world—has ceased to be at my death. True enough, but does it follow that in life my self-constituted world should become the world of everyone else as well? Obviously not, thinks Pascal; I may act as if this were the case in my relationships with other persons, but this is actually a self-deception caused by self-love, which warps and distorts both myself and my world. Three centuries later, Jean-Paul Sartre would arrive at a very similar analysis of human nature, but without the influence of that realistic and rigorous Christianity that animated Pascal's thought.

It is man's natural and necessary state that he should see the world from wherever he happens to be placed in it, so that no two individuals inhabit precisely the same world. But vanity makes a vice out of this necessity, says Pascal, by turning the very meaning of selfhood into something that feeds upon itself and makes itself its own object. The picture is a harsh one, but is it excessive or exaggerated? Is there nothing in human nature as such which can counteract and lessen the domineering pressure of self-love? If there is, Pascal seems to be unaware of it; and it can hardly be gainsaid that human selfhood with its "I, mine" does have a hateful aspect.

The ego of man, loving itself most and considering everything in terms of its own interests, long-range or immediate, therefore hates to learn the truth about itself:

> It conceives a mortal hatred of that truth which reproves and convicts its faults. . . . It takes great pains to cover up its faults both from others and from the self. . . . It is bad enough to be full of faults, but even worse to be full of them and yet unwilling to admit them. (E 99; P 978.)

The ego is inveterately egoistic and tries to cover up this truth. Pascal is saying what Saint Paul and Saint Augustine said before him and Sigmund Freud and Reinhold Niebuhr said after him. We not only deceive ourselves about ourselves but make every effort to deceive others. Society, the "earthly city," cannot exist without this mutual deceit: "I state it as a fact that if all men knew what others say of them behind their backs, there would not be four friends left in the world." (E 254; P 792.) We play the game of flattery in each other's presence on the basis of a tacit understanding that this is what everyone wants to hear, but as soon as we are separated the game is dropped and less amiable games begin.

One wishes that Pascal had distinguished sick self-love or *amour-propre* from the healthy *amour de soi* which is the very foundation of regard and sympathy for others, but he did not. What he has left us, however, is an unsparing view of man's inherent tendency toward "disguise, falsehood, hypocrisy"—in short, for self-deception. To cajole and butter up ourselves and others, from an overweening love of self, becomes the rule of life. Even more than the other deceiving powers, *vanité* reveals man at his desperate worst: "We run carelessly toward the precipice, after we have put something in front of us to keep ourselves from seeing it." (E 342; P 166.)

III

Although he can draw, with Daumier-like exactitude, a series of vignettes mirroring man's self-deceiving propensities, Pascal does not let us forget that he is a serious thinker intent upon discovering what being human means. Sooner or later, therefore, he must address himself to the familiar problem of the highest good for man. What is it that is ultimately good, through which all things derive their own goodness? His reflections on this subject, bound together in preparation for his writing of the Apology, are disappointing if one expects a chain of definitions and arguments in the classical tradition of ethics. Yet he does not forsake the tradition altogether, but joins Aristotle and the ancients in posing the problem of the supreme good in terms of the perennial question about human happiness. It can be taken for granted, he believes, that everyone wishes to be genuinely happy and acts with this aim in more or less constant view. However, no one seems to find what he or she is looking for, at least not permanently or truly.

"Our nature lies in movement; complete rest is death." Man's restlessness is a sure sign that he is seeking happiness without possessing it. But what is this goal that magnetizes so much of our longing and striving? There are two hundred and eighty sovereign goods for the philosophers, Pascal calculates with hasty sarcasm; but all these are various forms of happiness for man. The search for happiness is never-ending and exceedingly diverse, but very determined; it may as well be called a seeking after pleasure, in the broad Epicurean sense—pleasures old or new, lusty or lofty, solicited by a kind of perpetual motion set up in the human spirit. Do not all man's troubles, Pascal asks, come from the fact that it is impossible for any one of us to sit quietly in a single room for very long?

Man indeed wants happiness; but since he cannot bear honest, silent solitude, how can he ever recognize that he has what he needs in order to be truly happy? The cause of man's ingrained tendency toward distraction or *divertissement* is as simple as the forms it takes are devious and complex. *Divertissement* is as broad as human life itself, embracing beauty, pleasure, enjoyment, thought, action, love, and work. In all such seemingly random movements man is avoiding himself, turning away from his view of himself. In all the centuries of man-watching no one has looked at self-distraction more severely than Pascal. His picture of the king, who must surround himself with jesters and courtiers to avoid the necessity of coming to terms with himself as a human being, has a kind of classic force. It may be compared with Rouault's painting of the Old King, hardened and alone among the signs of his majesty.

The more man's efforts to find happiness end in failure, the more intense and frantic his diversionary tactics become. Put in contemporary language, his very activism can be just escapism. For lack of a genuine self to give, man gives away whatever he has of selfhood and dignifies his giving by calling it engagement or commitment. A preference for being where the action is can simply avoid *being* by confusing it with action. *Divertissement* has its source in man's self-contradiction as his desire for happiness perpetually defeats itself, but for that reason is perpetually renewed. In a trenchant essay on this Pascalian theme Henri Lefebvre relates it to self-alienation in the thought of Hegel and Marx.[37] But Pascal himself is not so ideological and theoretical. He is content to describe what he takes to be the human situation—to be sure, with what Lefebvre calls *la recherche implacable de la vérité*, but always eyeing the concrete and the variable aspects of his picture. Man, he holds, does not seek things so much as the search itself. He prefers the race to the prize, the hunt to the hare, the game to the victory. It is not the success that pleases him most, but the contest with its rivalry and excitement. "So we never really live but are always hoping to live, and as we are forever preparing for happiness it is inevitable that we are never really happy." (E 84; P 47.)

Such is the portrayal, in summary, that Pascal draws of man's misery, his wretchedness without God: a misfit in the universe, mistaking his emptiness for completeness, fleeing the truth in frenzied pursuit of nonexistent happiness. It is a sobering, even brutal picture: "The last act is tragic, no matter how pleasant the rest of the comedy. A handful of dirt is thrown on our heads, and *voilà* forever." (E 341; P 165.)

At this point, having reached bottom as it were, Pascal's thought takes a perhaps surprising turn. Leaving behind kaleidoscopic description and a kind of intuitive-clinical analysis, it becomes an argument. We may assume that here the first part of the Apology would have ended and the construction of a long "bridge" to the second part would begin. Pascal now declares that man's very misery, with its downward pull toward death, may serve as an image of man's true greatness. To be sure, it is a warped and distorted image, like the reflection one has of himself in a curved mirror at a carnival. But no candid effort at self-knowledge can ignore the fact that a true estimate of human greatness must move through, and not around, the full consideration of our common wretchedness. Some of Pascal's notes collected under the title *Grandeur* indicate this dialectical turning point:

> Man's grandeur is so evident that it can be inferred even from his misery. . . . The greatness of man is great in that he recognizes himself to be miserable. A tree does not know itself miserable. . . . Man's grandeur is proved by these very miseries. They are the miseries of a great lord, of a king dethroned. (E 221, 218, 220; P 117, 114, 116.)

Pascal's habit of thinking dialectically runs all through his work, but it is nowhere more in evidence than in his *portrait de l'homme*. A careful examination of his dialectical method must be postponed to a later chapter. As regards man, such a method is made necessary, Pascal holds, because of the contradictory nature of the subject. Having adopted for his purposes the familiar Renaissance maxim that man is *ni ange ni bête*, Pascal goes on to say, "and the pity of it is that in trying to act like an angel he only behaves like an animal" (E 257; P 678). Other examples of the same method come to mind:

> Man is only a reed, the feeblest thing in nature, but he is a *thinking* reed (*un roseau pensant*). There is no need for the entire universe to crush him by arming itself; a single vapor, one drop of water, is enough to kill him. But when the universe does crush him, man is still nobler than that which kills him, for he knows that he dies and knows the advantage the universe has over him, while the universe knows nothing of this.

> The pursuit of glory is man's worst baseness, yet it is also the chief sign of his excellence. (E 217, 91; P 200, 470.)

My existence as a man does not therefore tell a straight and simple story that is capable of being assumed and acted upon forthwith. Rather, it tells an extraordinarily involved and intricate story building to an unknown conclusion. The story of man, just because it is so full of *contrariétés*, warrants neither optimism nor pessimism. Such verdicts are opinions prompted by conflicting moods under the influence of good days or bad, as Pascal says; but each omits the other's necessary truth concerning man. The choice is not that between a high and a low understanding of what makes men and women human. Truth requires that we choose both, whatever one's predilections may be.

No single formula can cover the reality of being human, thinks Pascal. The true image of man must be at least a double one, as in this well-known paragraph:

> Quelle chimère est donc que l'homme! Quelle nouveauté, quel monstre, quel chaos, quel sujet de contradiction, quel prodige! Juge de toutes choses, imbécile ver de terre; dépositaire du vrai, cloaque d'incertitude et d'erreur; gloire et rebut de l'univers!
> (What sort of freak then is man! How novel, how monstrous, how chaotic, how contradictory, how prodigious! Judge of all things, imbecile earthworm, depository of truth, cesspool of doubt and error, the glory and refuse of the universe!) (E 246; P 131.)

Several features of the passage are noteworthy. Compact as it is, the exclamation groups together a series of images, each complete in itself, but exposing to view all the contradictory variety of which man is composed. Their profusion is condensed into a sharp antithesis that vibrates, despite its emphatic form, with questioning force. Pascal's rhetoric is clearly in a Renaissance vein, marked by the same excited sense of self-discovery, the same tendency toward hyperbole, that Shakespeare's "What a piece of work is a man!" speech in *Hamlet* contains. However, in Pascal's outburst the moods of astonishment and admiration are strongly tempered by a sense of man's grotesque, unreal, and vulnerable nature, preparing the way for Alexander Pope's *Essay on Man* with its distinct Pascalian echo:

> Chaos of thought and passion all confus'd;
> Still by himself abused or disabused;
> Created half to rise and half to fall;
> Great lord of all things, yet a prey to all;
> Sole judge of truth, in endless error hurled;
> The glory, jest, and riddle of the world!

Knowing the truth about man, then, is both necessary and salutary in Pascal's view. It means taking seriously the paradoxical, self-contradictory character of everything human. How is such knowledge possible, though, when man as such is said to be incapable of it, liable to error and uncertainty in all respects? In particular, how can Pascal himself, as human as the next man, presume to have this needed truth? Has he not already given an interpretation of the human situation that renders any remedy he offers highly suspect? Since questions like these are bound to occur to Pascal's readers it is fair to assume that they must have arisen in his mind as well.

One may fault Pascal for not answering such questions as they come up, but rightly or wrongly his strategy in the projected Apology requires that the reader should remain in suspense a while longer. The dialectical balance now established between *misère* and *grandeur* must be maintained, at least temporarily. Meanwhile it is better to accept contradiction where one finds it than to try to gloss it over by generalized simplifications as false as they may be plausible. In any case the human situation does not forbid, but rather demands, that man should keep on searching for the truth about himself.

Indeed, it is the search for truth, made possible by thought, which counterbalances man's wretchedness. Pascal writes: "All our dignity consists in thought. . . . Let us labor then to think well. . . . It is thought which constitutes the greatness of man." (E 232; P 756.) Clearly, this is said to man's credit and for his encouragement. It should nevertheless be noticed that when Pascal asserts that "man is visibly made to think" he does not simply repeat Descartes's more famous statement, "I think, therefore I am." To Pascal, thought is not so much the defining as the *dignifying* element in human nature. He regards it more as a capacity to be exercised and fulfilled than as an innate faculty that is self-intuited and self-possessed. Its worth depends entirely on what use is made of it, what its objects and intentions are.

Philosophers such as Miguel de Unamuno and Bertrand

Russell have taken Pascal severely to task for holding such an equivocal view of the powers of human intelligence. It is all very well, they argue, to praise man's rational capacity as Pascal seems to do; but what comes of it when his chief interest appears to be that of pointing to the failures and abuses of reason? If man is actually as wretched as he is portrayed in the *Pensées*, what good can come of declaring that his dignity consists in thought?

True, Pascal does not have utter confidence in reason, if this means relying upon logical methods and intellectual resources alone for reaching the whole truth about human life. He knew as well as Marx or Freud that reasoning may easily become mere rationalizing, making the worse appear the better reason. Nevertheless he insists on giving thought its due as the best instrument man has for seeking truth. Whatever else Pascal's position on the use of reason may be, it is not irrationalism. His picture of "the parrot, always wiping its beak even though it is clean" emphasizes the crucial difference between repetitive behavior in animals and rational behavior in man. His distinction, in the Preface to the Treatise on the Vacuum, between human progress in science and the instinctual behavior of bees in a hive makes a similar point. If a mechanical calculator performs arithmetical operations more efficiently than the human brain, that is because reason planned it that way. The classical Western tradition that man is a rational animal is obviously safe with Pascal.

Thus, while the fact that man is made to think affords no guarantee of immunity from the ills that mortal flesh is heir to, it does mean that the human situation is dynamically if ambiguously open. Just how open may be judged from Pascal's other statement that man is not made but for infinity, which, as we shall see, illumines many Pascalian themes and issues. In Pascal's mind there is a natural affinity between thinking and the infinite—"natural" in the sense that thought, with all its built-in liabilities, is still the human point of contact with whatever is beyond or above the human. Man's greatness then is real and not illusory, but it consists in a direction or dimension of his existence rather than in anything he can be said to possess and control. Reading Pascal on man, one is reminded of George Herbert's words:

> Unless he can above himself erect himself
> How poor a thing is man!

IV

If there is one word that catches up better than another the spirit of Pascal's reflections on man, it is the word *coeur,* or heart. His frequent and emphatic use of this term places him within the company of poets and mystics rather than philosophers and scientists. Indeed, it expresses his own choice of the *esprit de finesse,* contrasted with the *esprit géométrique,* for inquiring into distinctly human matters.

The Dictionary of the French Academy, first published in 1694, lists no less than fifteen current meanings of the word *coeur.* It may signify the vital principle in animals, the seat of the passions, the upper opening of the stomach, as well as courage, force, vigor, affection, thought, memory, or "the center of something." Evidently it was a remarkably vague and versatile term then as now. In Pascal's hands, however, the word takes on a resonance that is quite unique.

Since *coeur* has a pivotal importance in the Pascalian view of man its range of meaning should be carefully indicated. First, the reader of Pascal must be cautioned that he does not mean by "the heart" what Romantic writers of the nineteenth century have taught us to mean by it. We shall misread him if we take *coeur* as simply a synonym for instinct over against intelligence, or for emotion as opposed to reason. While he clearly intends to convey by it "the feeling side of life" he does not use it to exclude or disparage something called "the mind." Indeed, in Pascal's usage, the heart has much to do with mental effort and intellectual discovery. One may find suggestive comparisons in other writers, notably Cardinal Newman's "intimate understanding" or Bergson's "intuition."

Secondly, the adoption of this word by Pascal reveals how

greatly he was influenced by the language of Scripture. In the Psalms, for example, the heart is taken to mean the center from which a person feels, thinks, or acts, his most inward and hidden self. It is not a symbol for any part of man, not even the highest or noblest part, but the living whole of man grasped in moments of intense, honest self-transparency. Ordinarily, to be sure, a man does not know his own heart, because of the strength of the *puissances trompeuses;* but God sees the heart and speaks directly to it in either grace or judgment. From the Biblical and Christian point of view, that which "makes a man tick" is the potential locus of self-knowledge and redemptive contact with God who sees in secret who man really is; yet the heart is also where man's deception and disloyalty originate, the source of subterfuge or evasion. The heart is where man lives although it may not be where man is most at home. All through the Bible, underscored by prophets and apostles, highlighted especially in the teaching of Jesus, this meaning of the heart as the personal center of awareness and response, ambivalent or authentic as the case may be, is present. Pascal's writing on man is marked by the same Biblical accent.

Thirdly, it is worth observing that Pascal, here as elsewhere, does not construct a technical vocabulary for his special purposes but is content to use words as they arise in common speech. He takes them as he finds them, with the very real risk that he may be misunderstood, because he wishes to engage his reader in conversation about matters that are of common and crucial concern. In moving from science and technology into humane studies, Pascal did not abandon exactness of expression; on the contrary, he seems to have had a rare gift for saying just what he intended. His use of the symbol of the heart, that greatly distended organ, reflects the fact that the nature and purpose of his inquiry have changed, and that a different mode of communication is required.

The best way to approach this basic Pascalian motif is by examining the *pensées* in which it prominently occurs. The most familiar is the one that begins: "The heart has its reasons which reason cannot know." (E 224; P 423.) This is not an opinion but an observation; Pascal has simply noticed in himself and others that the "reasons" which are given for behavior are usually not the "reasons" which in fact produce it. As it stands, the sentence makes the obvious, but easily overlooked, point that the explanations people advance for what they do are often at variance with the motives by which they are actually controlled. But what saves this observation from becoming a mere truism is Pascal's deliberate use of the single word "reason" in two very different senses joined compactly in what seems an arresting paradox. Common speech, which habitually confuses explanations with motives, is here corrected from within itself.

However, Pascal's own motive in writing this famous sentence lies at a still deeper level. He is saying that the heart, namely, one's inmost self, precedes and determines every kind of reason. This is the precise reversal of Descartes's *cogito ergo sum;* Pascal holds that I do not constitute myself by thought alone since my thinking self is basically the same as my desiring, willing, acting self. My thought, like everything else I am or do, has its secret springs in my interior *me.*

Oddly enough perhaps it is Pascal's emphasis upon the heart that keeps him from the antirationalism with which he is sometimes unfairly charged. If he directs attention to the fact that man is more than he knows, or permits others to know, it is in order that the fully *human* character of reason in its diverse forms may be recognized and appreciated. The Biblical statement that "as a man thinks in his heart, so is he" harmonizes exactly with Pascal's own. In neither case is there the slightest suggestion of a cynical irrationalism. Man, after all, is *made* to think; but he should be warned against thinking that his thought somehow exempts him from having to struggle with his own all-too-human nature. Man's dignity as a thinking being is not lessened but celebrated in this well-known *pensée* which holds, again with the Bible, that "out of the heart are the issues of life."

Another *pensée* dealing with the heart is this: "We know truth not by reason only, but by the heart." (E 214; P 110.) Pascal is referring here to his view that all demonstrative or analytical knowledge rests back upon the direct apprehension, feeling, and intellect involved together, of what he insists upon calling "first principles." In several of his notes Pascal gives more than a suggestion of his belief that unless these principles—space, time, number, and the like—are intuited, or felt-seen by the heart, there can be nothing at all to think about. These intuited principles, which Immanuel Kant was later to call "categories," are what all rational understanding must assume but cannot prove.

Yet once again Pascal goes deeper. His concern is not only to show that understanding begins necessarily with principles or forms of which we are immediately aware; he points out that we must trust our fundamental intuitions, put ourselves at their disposal for the sake of truth. Really to know something is to give oneself to it, follow its lead, let it shape and guide one's thought. Only so can man ever hope to remove sterile dualisms contrived by "reason alone" in order to excuse its failure to arrive at truth—those between object and subject, reality and appearance, world and self. Something like sympathy or rapport is at the core of every act of knowing the truth, and the word *coeur* is therefore appropriate for describing it. Once more a contrast with Descartes becomes inevitable; whereas he held that our existence is defined as rational, Pascal's view is that our reason is through and through existential.

Saint Augustine had made essentially the same point long before Pascal. Neither could conceive of man except as a truth-seeking being. Man needs truth in order to be himself, that is, to live humanely—honestly, fulfillingly, reasonably. But the attainment of truth depends upon that double movement of self-awareness and self-giving which for a Christian thinker is the inner rhythm of a fully human existence. Pascal's word "heart" signifies that rhythm, beating in harmony with the nature of things, which Augustine had expressed in the phrase *Non intratur in veritatem misi per caritatem* (There is no entering into truth except by way of love).

Nevertheless Pascal warns us not to think too highly of the heart: "How hollow and full of trash (*ordure*) is the heart of man!" (E 272; P 139.) Truth and love do not come naturally to man in his fallen state. This *pensée* recalls the prophet Jeremiah's lament:

> The heart is deceitful above all things, and desperately corrupt; who can understand it? "I the Lord search the mind and try the heart, to give to every man according to his ways, according to the fruit of his doings." (Jer. 17: 9–10.)

The most "real" thing about man may turn out to be his unreality, his heart's devious and self-deceiving way of fooling him about his actual goals, needs, powers, limitations. Do I love someone else chiefly because I love myself more, because I love being loved? Or when engaged in study and reflection is it really knowledge and learning I am after, or only status and security? The answer lies only within the heart of man, and since the heart is an inveterate trickster it must be laid bare and tested in the searching gaze of God. So Pascal believed.

If, then, man's heart is to be rescued from illusion and grasped instead by liberating truth, a structure of meaning and value capable of illuminating and enabling life from within will have to be found. The heart must be humbled, gentled, and opened by faith. Thus the misery of man without God will make way for the greatness of man with God, as Pascal puts it. He writes: "It is the heart which feels God, not the reason. This then is faith: God felt by the heart, not by the reason." (E 225; P 424.) *Dieu sensible au coeur*—these words were much admired and quoted by the close of the seventeenth century; Madame de Sévigné, for instance, mentions them in a letter written in 1692.

The import of these words has often been discussed by Pascalian scholars from that day to our own. In an excellent, inclusive study of Pascal's view Jean Laporte has written:

> If there is a legitimate place at all for the heart and its reasons,
> it is because reason does not exhaust either reality or the
> knowledge we have of reality. It is because reason is not enough
> for man, and perhaps not enough even for itself.[38]

Granted, Laporte's interest here is mainly that of pointing
out the deficiencies of reason, which is of lesser interest to
Pascal himself. It is clear, he thinks, that while reason may
form ideas of God it cannot by itself experience God; only
the heart—man in his centered selfhood—can do that. And
yet the work of reason in the service of the heart is indispensable. To what other human capacity can we look for that
rigorous pruning of preconceptions, that astringent cleansing
of willful ignorance and error, that can free the heart for
love and truth? Pascal exhibits little patience with those who
would disparage reason in order to make room for faith. But
he knows, and not least from his own experience, that it is
the heart, embracing and moving the reason, which must
respond to God as the truth. A God unloved is a God unknown. And it must be God himself who awakens the sensibility of faith within the heart of man.

V

A present-day philosopher, Henri Lefebvre, Marxist by allegiance and conviction, has confessed that he reads Pascal on
man with a kind of "holy horror." This view of man, he
holds, is doubtless fascinating; indeed, it devours, burns, and
consumes the reader of Pascal; but it must be thrown off and
rejected once for all.[39] He speaks for many others who assert
that they have been likewise disquieted and repelled by Pascal's
portrait of the misery and grandeur of the human condition.

Perhaps, indeed, Pascal did his work too well. It may be
that his description of man is but a masterpiece of grim
overstatement. He is so adept at puncturing the balloons of
pretense and vanity, so insistent on exposing self-deception
and self-justification, that it is easy to conclude that he is
more concerned to pillory man's wretchedness than to celebrate

his greatness, whatever he may claim to the contrary. At all events many have thought and said so.

There is, however, another possible explanation for the prevalence of this widely shared impression that Pascal is somehow *against* man. Its causes may lie more within the reader than the author. Let it be admitted that temperamental affinities or ideological commitments do make it difficult for Pascal to reach us. Some regard Pascal's overly realistic portrayal as a kind of solemn joke not to be taken seriously, laced as it is with so much satire and apparent ridicule. Others, just because they agree with a great deal that Pascal says concerning man, are encouraged thereby to believe that it does not apply to themselves. They parry the force of the Pascalian dialectic precisely by accepting it theoretically as privileged knowledge which confirms them in feeling superior to the majority of mankind. Yet a person's reluctance to see himself in the Pascalian mirror may not necessarily be due to a fault in the mirror, especially when it has been constructed for the purpose of showing man trying not to see himself.

As Pascal would say, if man cannot bear to acknowledge his own wretchedness, how can he ever come to perceive his greatness? Yet if he is unable to accept his true greatness what is the point in facing his wretchedness?

Man's greatness is undeniable, for Pascal, and it consists in the fact that man is made for infinity. This may be termed the *idée maitresse* of all Pascalian thought. The theme is announced and rendered in many variations from the scientific to the religious. Man, alone in the universe, is a self-surpassing being who concerns himself with matters that take him out of himself and seeks his good beyond and above himself: *"L'homme passe infiniment l'homme."* (E 242; P 131.) His thought cannot come to rest in anything less than infinity, which is why he alternates so pathetically between *divertissement* and *ennui*. Hence man's misery "proves" his grandeur, since it is the sign of a self-transcending openness that only the infinite can satisfy.

Granted, this is a strange kind of greatness, quite unlike the *éclat* that surrounds a king, a general, an archbishop, or even a *savant*. It is defined not in terms of prestige bestowed by one's fellows, nor even in terms of an honor earned by one's own efforts; it has to do, rather, with man's nature as such. And yet man's greatness consists less in possession than in orientation; it is signaled by the presence of an absence, by a consciousness of what he lacks and needs to realize his own humanity. Man is great not in spite of the predicament and pathos that mark his existence but precisely by virtue of them. By thought he encompasses the universe that surrounds him, and he persists in his attempt to think what is unthinkable. He cannot recognize his liabilities without regretting them and wishing to surpass them. Thus he is always more than the mere sum of his experiences and relationships, more than his striving and seeking, more than he can ever know himself to be. He is great because his very humanity cannot be accounted for in terms of itself but fronts upon the infinite, as the shore both receives and holds back the ocean.

Is all this to be dismissed as sheer paradox and self-contradiction on Pascal's part? Hardly, for the greatness he attributes to man cannot even be denied without being confirmed, as it is in man's diversions and excursions themselves. What in animals we call nature, writes Pascal, is called wretchedness in man. A wealth of meaning is packed into this single observation. Its point is not to distinguish man from the subhuman, like Aristotle and his philosophical successors, including Descartes who defined man as the animal who reasons, laughs, makes tools, speaks, etc. Pascal's concern is with man's greatness, not his genus. He writes with a purpose that is neither comparative nor objective but frankly and inwardly persuasive. His point is that man's very humanity is constituted by his accessibility to the infinite for which he is created.

This view that man is great not because of something that belongs to him but by virtue of something to which he belongs can be recognized as directly dependent on the Biblical and Christian belief that man is created in the image of God. Pascal sketches in the already fading colors on the Christian canvas with fresh, bold strokes so that it becomes a truly modern statement. As he puts it, man is great enough to be called God's image, but has faults enough to be reminded that he is only God's image, neither more nor less.

The Pascalian understanding of what it means to be human may be sharpened by comparing it with the writings of Albert Camus in our own century. The comparison is appropriate since Camus acknowledged Pascal's influence upon his view. Both men saw clearly the tragic dimension of man's existence and made no effort to explain away the facts of moral and natural evil. Camus, in particular, denied the charges of pessimism and defeatism leveled by critics against his work, holding up the possibility of heroic human effort in the face of what he termed the absurdity of existence. Man can, like Sisyphus in the ancient myth, keep on performing a frustrating and meaningless task. Like Dr. Rieux in Camus's *The Plague* he can express in action his solidarity with the helpless victims of catastrophic disease. And, unlike Jean-Baptiste Clemence in *The Fall,* he can answer a fellow human being's cry for help when it reaches him. At least he may do nothing to add voluntarily to the misery of existence, and in his own person he can revolt against it.

Camus and Pascal are in remarkable agreement that man's absurd or self-contradictory state need not immobilize him on a dead center of despair. The difference, however, is also great, and it is made by Christian faith. Camus, convinced that Christianity promises a way out of human meaninglessness which it cannot produce, urges heroic resistance without hope of victory now or hereafter. Pascal, on the contrary, would find such groundless courage even more absurd than the absurdity it fights against. Not that he has a better "answer" than Camus does to the mystery of evil; but Pascal believes that man's extremity is God's opportunity.

Self-fulfillment is not a simple human possibility; and to know this is enough to make man miserable—without God.

Nevertheless, what makes misery really miserable is that it is a deprivation, a felt absence or an aching void. Hence Pascal's insightful question: "For who is unhappy over not being king, except a dethroned king?" (E 221; P 117.) Here, of course, another Christian theme comes to the fore, that of the fall of man from an original wholeness and blessedness. But this means, again, that man's wretchedness is the sign of his authentic greatness. This is so in the same sense that darkness has no meaning except in terms of light, or evil except in terms of good, or error except in terms of truth. Since man's behavior does not exemplify his God-given being, he must be remade in the likeness of the infinite for which he has been made.

Pascal's explorations into human nature can be understood as an articulate whole despite their fragmentary character in the *Pensées*. His notes on this subject are frequently among the most carefully written and revised of all those intended for the Apology that was never finished. It is clear moreover that what gives to Pascal's thought concerning man its notable spaciousness and coherence is its Christian *provenance*. He wishes by his own admission to make man comprehensible to himself. Several of his *pensées* on "order" indicate the strategy he meant to follow in developing his argument. Anyone is at liberty to pick his view of man to pieces, objecting to this or that assertion, pitting one opinion against another. To do so, however, is to lose the thread of a consistent and cumulative argument.

Pascal evidently had no intention of putting forward an interpretation of man on purely non-Christian grounds, to which he then might offer some kind of "Christian answer." His view of man's misery is as Christian as his proposals for overcoming it. If his strategy moves from misery to grandeur, the substance of his thought—the structure of his argument— moves the other way around. But it is equally wide of the mark to assume that Pascal gives a "Christian" (and therefore outgrown and dismissable) analysis for which some better contemporary or secular substitute must be found. Pascal on man is obviously no pastiche or period piece.

A full justification of this estimate must wait upon the next chapter. But enough has been said here to indicate that Pascal is a Christian humanist *par excellence*. To be sure, he stands more in the tradition of Saint Augustine, Dante, or Milton than in that of Clement, Abelard, or Erasmus. One of the foremost Pascalian scholars of an earlier generation, who also was a renowned student of Montaigne, was Fortunat Strowski. He wrote that it was Pascal's belief that Christianity, after having laid bare the enigma of human nature, brings forward the true remedy for man's ailments. In the chapter that follows, the truth of this belief is to be examined and assessed.

4. The Believer

Many students of Pascal have remarked upon the abrupt, impetuous quality of his thought and life. His zest for discovering truth was so great, punctuated as it was by intermittent illness, that he often interrupted work on one project to turn to another. Perhaps all works of genius are leaps of this kind, as the poet Novalis declared. In Pascal's case this characteristic abruptness and high mobility kept him from being captivated by any partial truth while maintaining his freedom for new explorations.[40]

At the same time Pascal could consolidate the gains already made in one phase of his work as he moved on to the next. From science and invention he acquired a respect for facts and rational clarity which he carried into all his subsequent inquiries and reflections. From the study of human conduct and character he derived a keen perception of the fragile splendor of existence which nourished his deepening religious interest and commitment. Indeed, he believed his lifelong search for truth was satisfied in faith. "There are three kinds of persons," he observes,

> those who serve God, having found him; others who are busy seeking him, not having found him; and still others who live without either seeking him or finding him. The first are reasonable and happy; the last are foolish and unhappy; those in between are unhappy, but reasonable. (E 336; P 160.)

Here Pascal is saying that "finding God," the life-in-faith, neither contradicts nor endangers the fulfillment that every person seeks; he would not commend faith unless it yielded the advantage of a reasonable happiness. That is required by his realistic assessment of the human situation. It does not mean, however, that faith should be embraced merely for its intellectual and practical benefits. Although man is always a creature named desire, he is also made for infinity and cannot come to rest in anything less. Hence faith, in Pascal's thought, remains a leap attended with great risks, but a leap well worth the taking for the truth and well-being it bestows.

I

When his personal development is considered, it is understandable that Pascal gave close attention to what philosophers and theologians call the faith-reason problem. Moreover, this was also one of the significant problems of his own century, made both acute and urgent by the accelerated tempo of scientific discovery as well as by the emergence of new options in religion. Traditionalism was on the defensive all along the cultural front. New views of the world and of the human person, revolutionary in their implications for faith and knowledge alike, were much in evidence. The Reformation and the Counter-Reformation both brought forth more radical, austere demands on behalf of Christianity which were met with every kind of response ranging from skeptical disdain to deepened institutional loyalty and heightened private spirituality. Pascal felt and indeed lived at the juncture of these tensions and challenges, fully aware of the momentous issues at stake for himself and his time.

His own thought on this particular problem of the relationship between reason and faith was far from static. The first reference to it occurs in his Preface to the Treatise on the Vacuum, where he objects to the frequent use by scientists of appeals to authority and antiquity. Pascal believes that in science, methods of exact observation and controlled experiment should be the only court of appeal. In other words, scientific questions must have scientific answers, not metaphysical or theological ones. By the same token, questions of Christian truth need to be dealt with by the canons of the historic faith; hence one has every right to appeal to established tradition and the testimony of its authoritative witnesses. The point is that Pascal will not accept either dogmatism in science or rationalism in religion. The two realms of truth must be treated separately. He wishes to rid faith of superstition as well as to purge science of pseudo-theological assumptions. What he envisages is a commonsense, clear-cut division of labor that frees each sphere from encroachment or interference by the other.

In the eighteenth Provincial Letter he returns to the faith-reason problem in the context of his defense of the Jansenists who had been charged with heresy by the Jesuits. Throughout the *Letters* his strategy has been to show that the question of whether an opinion is heretical or not is one to be decided by proper church authority; but the question of whether someone actually holds such an opinion is simply one of fact to be determined by examining the relevant materials. Here he reminds his Jesuit antagonist of the traditional distinctions:

> How then do we learn the truth regarding facts? From our eyes, Father, which are the rightful judges of fact, as reason is of natural and intelligible things, and faith of supernatural and revealed things . . . these three principles of our knowledge each have separate objects, and certainty within that range. . . . Matters of fact can only be proved by the senses.

Hence, as Pascal says, even popes are liable to be taken off guard; and he adds with wry humor that the church's condemnation of Galileo as a heretic was unable to keep the earth from turning, or all the people in the world from turning with it. "Not all the powers on earth can, by force of authority, persuade us of a point of fact, any more than they can change it; for nothing can make non-existent something that really is." [41]

Although Pascal does not deal in this letter with the full dimensions of the faith-reason problem as such, he professes to be thoroughly orthodox with reference to the matter at hand. That is, he bases his attack on the traditional, official distinction between faith and reason as it had been set forth by Saint Thomas Aquinas. He agrees in principle with Thomas and the Council of Trent that faith is above reason but not contrary to reason. Nevertheless the effect of his argument is to unsettle the Thomistic solution to the problem. How, for instance, can Pascal accept the view that faith and reason do not have the same object, when he holds that it would destroy faith if doubt were cast on the evidence of the senses? When a text for possible heresy is examined, the criteria of factual observation, rational consistency, and doctrinal correctness all come into play. Thus faith does not determine its own truth by a method peculiar to itself, even though Pascal insists upon its right to do so.

The faith-reason problem, after all, is the problem of a relationship and not of sheer difference; otherwise there would be no problem. Saint Thomas himself had written that there can be no final opposition between truths of the natural intelligible and the supernatural-revealed kind, though in practice they should be kept distinct. In the seventeenth century the Thomistic solution was still very much in force, although coming under increased pressure from the rationalists, of whom Descartes may be taken as a leading protagonist. Descartes repeats the scholastic formulas distinguishing three kinds of questions: those things believed by faith because of revelation such as the Trinity or the incarnation; those which pertain to faith but are also open to rational confirmation, such as the existence of God or the distinction between soul and body; and finally those belonging to determination by reason alone, such as squaring the circle or the chemical formula for producing gold. However Thomistic this may appear on the surface, Descartes's real interest lies in emphasizing the absolute power of reason both as leading to faith and as recognizing its supplementation by faith.

Pascal, on the contrary, finds no such compatibility based on rational continuity possible. Though he also uses the traditional distinctions he adds the level of observed fact to the others and regards it as fundamental to both. If at this stage of his thought he is more confused than Descartes, it is because he is in search of a method more complex, pliable, and profound. The faith-reason problem is posed for Pascal in a variety of ways: tradition versus novelty (the exchange with Père Noël), authority versus freedom in both science and religion, dogmatism versus empiricism (whether in theology masquerading as science or in so-called science presuming to define or limit the truth of faith). In each case he chooses to be a believing thinker, or thinking believer—to be faithful and reasonable, both at once, not one at the expense of the other. But he would be the last to say that such an aim can be pursued without real strain and conflict that may seriously impair man's whole vision of the truth.

In those *pensées* destined for the Apology which touch upon the faith-reason problem Pascal's further reflection is expressed. A large part of his notes on the matter were collected under the title "Submission and Use of Reason." Here is an especially pithy one:

> The final step of reason is to acknowledge that there is an infinity of things which go beyond it. It is weak indeed if it cannot go far enough to understand that. (E 373; P 188.)

There are others in similar vein:

> Nothing is so congruous with reason as this disavowal of reason.

> Saint Augustine. Reason would never submit unless it judged that there are times when it ought to do so. Therefore it is right that it should submit when it judges that it ought to do so.

> Two extremes—to exclude reason, to admit nothing but reason. (E 367, 359, 368; P 182, 174, 183.)

On the one hand, Pascal's thought seems to be quite in accord with the accepted Thomist solution to the problem. While reason can never produce faith it may prepare the way for faith. To believe is certainly not the same as to know, and yet it is essential to know when believing is required. Hence reason has a crucial function in deciding what belongs to faith, as Descartes had insisted.

In several other respects, however, these *pensées* do not reflect the Cartesian or Thomistic positions at all. First, Pascal has stated the case for reason in a characteristically ironic, paradoxical manner; the highest exercise of reason is said to be its self-surrender or "submission" when it knows its limits have been reached, so that its very impotence becomes its triumph. Second, one finds no support here for the view shared by Descartes with the Thomistic tradition that reason is able to prove some of the truths of faith. The idea of a "natural theology" is repugnant to Pascal, partly because he thinks it involves an unwarranted confusion of categories and methods, partly because it does not acknowledge the significant role played by the *heart* in preparing man for both reason and faith. The stars and the birds do not "prove God," says Pascal, and even if they did, it would not be the God of living faith but some hypothetical abstraction invoked to get reason out of its own difficulties.

Nevertheless, it would be unjust to Pascal to suppose that he dealt only negatively with the problem. Actually he speaks out of a much richer and older tradition than either modern rationalism or medieval Scholasticism when he writes of faith and reason. He evokes the teaching of Saint Augustine, sharpened by Anselm of Canterbury, that faith itself pursues understanding, *fides quaerens intellectum*. Faith like reason is in search of an ever fuller truth. Although no amount of reasoning can yield one ounce of faith, reason can—once faith is present and active—set itself to *comprehend* what faith admittedly can only *apprehend*. When thinking becomes believing it does not cease to think; what it gives up is the presumption that thought can determine reality, or that everything worth knowing can be reached by logical and rational methods alone.

If Pascal seems to lay undue stress upon the dangers and

temptations in reasoning that gets out of its depth and will not acknowledge real and irreducible mystery, this is because he was well acquainted with intellectual pride in himself and others. As he worked his way through the faith-reason problem, Pascal more and more abandoned the effort to give each its due and emphasized the primacy, rather than the autonomy or superiority, of faith to reason. With typical dialectical skill he sees reason becoming perfected in vulnerability, in that openness to what is beyond or above it which he termed both the use and the submission of reason. Augustinian that he is, he maintains that truth is one and indivisible, calling forth the complementary though not interchangeable responses of reasonable and faithful man.

Everything that is written on this subject in the *Pensées* should be read with Pascal's personal experience and intellectual growth in mind: his long apprenticeship to experimental and mathematical science, his discovery of man, his decisive conversion to "the God of Abraham, Isaac, and Jacob, not the God of the philosphers and the *savants*." He had been led to encounter an infinity of things that go beyond reason, he became keenly aware of the reasons of the heart, and therefore also of the need for faith which believes where it cannot claim to know. Still, he did not on that account reject or despise reason, but continued to employ it faithfully in a life increasingly illuminated by Scripture and set within the discipline and devotion of the visible church.

II

In the light of his own development, therefore, it is not surprising that Pascal should have conceived its meaning as a successive exposure to zones of being, "Orders" as he called them, which are not merely gradations in an ascending scale of values but represent real breaks and leaps within discovered truth as well. The idea had been growing in Pascal's mind for some time; intimations may be found in his letter to Queen Christina, in his mathematical work on the summation of powers, in his short essays *L'Esprit Géométrique* and *L'Art de Persuader,* and elsewhere. This memorable passage in the *Pensées* formulates the theme of the Orders most succinctly:

> The infinite distance between bodies and minds is a symbol of the infinitely more infinite distance between minds and charity, for charity is more than natural. . . . All the *éclat* of high rank has no splendor for those whose pursuits are intellectual. The greatness of men of intellect is invisible to kings, to the rich, to captains, and to all the worldly great. The greatness of wisdom, which is nothing unless it comes from God, is invisible to the worldly and to intellectuals. These are three orders different in kind. . . . All bodies, the firmament, the stars, the earth and its kingdoms are not equal to the least of minds, for mind knows them all and itself, while they know nothing. All bodies together, and all minds together, with all their productions, are not equal to the slightest motion of charity; that is of an infinitely higher order. From all bodies together one little thought cannot be obtained. That is impossible; thought belongs to a different order. From all bodies and minds not one feeling of true charity can be produced. That is impossible, of another order, supernatural. (E 585; P 308.)

This page, which some have judged the finest written in the French language, is a fitting introduction to Pascal's experience and view of the transcendent, which for him made possible the right ordering of his entire existence as a thinking, believing man.

Cultured Europeans at this time took pretty much for granted the notion of a separation between bodily and mental events, parallel to but independent of each other, or else interacting through some mysterious juncture such as the pineal gland which Descartes located as the point of contact. Pascal evidently accepted the current parallelism without question, having neither interest nor experimental knowledge in matters of physiology. He does not seem to have been acquainted with William Harvey's epoch-making discovery of the circulation of the blood, although it was made during his own lifetime.

Another generally accepted distinction during this period was that between the natural and the supernatural. In the form in which Pascal received it, the concept of the supernatural referred mainly to such acts of God as miracle or revelation, even though these actions were effected in and through the natural order of physical causation and rational knowledge. This distinction was developed chiefly by theologians and philosophers of the later Middle Ages who found that they had to reckon with the rediscovery of Aristotle and the impact of Jewish and Islamic thought. Confronted by sophisticated forms of paganism, they endeavored to validate in this way the distinctive superiority of Christian truth. As a scientist Pascal is much intrigued by this idea, but adapts it to his own purposes with considerable freedom, especially in writing about miracles.

Superimposing these two fundamental distinctions, Pascal humanizes and Christianizes them, in order to fashion not a metaphysical or theological doctrine at all, but rather a more adequate *perspective* for seeing man in his twofold relationship to nature and to God. The three orders are ways of ordering human existence; taken together they constitute a notable effort on Pascal's part to give meaningful coherence and direction to that existence. The whole perspective thus established is kept dynamically open at both ends of the spectrum of reality which it embraces, indicated by the fact that Pascal's designation for the orders is not uniform or fixed. Hence the order of charity is also termed that of the will or the heart, while that of bodies includes not simply physical matter but what Saint Paul called "the flesh," which means life organized on the basis of self-interest as if there were no God. The order of minds is designated by the word *esprit*— really untranslatable into English—with overtones of meaning running all the way from "spirit" to "intelligence" not unrelated to "wit." This last, Pascal thinks, is man's unique order although he participates in the others as well by virtue of his mysteriously compound and open nature.

The history of Western philosophy includes some noteworthy attempts to map the structure of reality by constructing a scale of beings from the lowest to the highest. In particular, Neoplatonism in a Christianized, Augustinian form entered into medieval and modern thought to such a degree that Pascal was clearly influenced by it; but the three orders do not properly belong to this tradition. Although they are inconceivable without reference to the "great chain of being," they are not a further metaphysical scheme to subdivide and synthesize reality. In Pascal's century Cardinal Bérulle made just such an effort, pretentious and hollow, which is now all but forgotten. Instead, what Pascal proposes is a bright thread leading through the labyrinth of human experience, a telling clue for ordering and seeing rightly what would otherwise seem at best confusing, at worst absurd. As soon as his conception has been hardened by interpretation into some kind of cosmic stepladder, its whole point has been lost.

Nevertheless the three orders must be taken seriously as Pascal presents them, namely as giving important insight into man's whole being-in-the-world, rather than as a playful by-product of Pascal's flair for sheer invention. Each order is best described as a particular sense of value with its own focus of interest, kind of obstacle or temptation, and quality of response. Taken together the orders throw into relief an ascending and descending hierarchy of experienced worth: the first is that of manipulative power based on force, the second that of intellectual achievement based on reasoning, the third that of willing and loving self-donation based on faith in God as Jesus Christ reveals him.

It is significant that Pascal's thought refuses to pluralize or synthesize the orders; here as elsewhere he remains true to his fundamental dialectical principle that "everything is one, everything is different." Each order is one way of ordering or valuing the whole of experience, not a segment, phase, or stage within that wholeness. Each is discontinuous and *sui generis* with respect to the others. Nevertheless, each has its own internal complexity as well. For example, the *ordre de la chair* or material greatness includes the physical universe, the life of animals, and that aspect of human life in which "concupiscence properly rules"; Pascal never makes entirely clear the affinity between material things and carnal appetites, and the picture may be complicated still further by including scientific knowledge (of *les choses sensibles*) under the order of *esprit*. But the values of each order are peculiar to it, even if the realities to which they are attached show up again, transvalued, in another order. In the long *pensée* we are considering, Pascal gives some illuminating examples. Archimedes, though of princely rank, had no need to play the prince to command respect in his own domain of science; and the same is true of Jesus Christ. Pascal writes:

> It would have been pointless for our Lord Jesus Christ to come with splendor as a king in his reign of holiness, yet he came indeed with splendor in his own order! It is quite absurd to be scandalized at the lowliness of Jesus, as if his lowliness were of the same order as the greatness he came to reveal. (E 585; P 308.)

Thus there is an order among the orders—striking liaisons and dependences appears as well as necessary differences. For Pascal, contrast is always a form of coherence; unless truth *is*, nothing can be true, not even the tiniest tremor of the senses. Although there is an infinite distance between the orders, it is only the structure of relationships among them which makes this distance understandable. Pascal conceives the structure to be hierarchical, that is, determined from above downward rather than from below upward. A lower order cannot generate a higher, but a higher order includes a lower by virtue of its very superiority to it. Indeed all the lower orders, however diverse and apparently autonomous, derive their very ordering from *charité,* which is the substance of God's self-disclosure of himself as the Truth in which all truths finally converge.

Always an Augustinian thinker, Pascal reveals his allegiance in the following *pensée* suggested by the reading of I John 2:16:

> "Concupiscence of the flesh, concupiscence of the eyes, pride," etc. There are three orders of things: flesh, intelligence, and will.

The carnal are the rich and kings. The body is their object.
The curious and learned: their object is the mind.
The wise: they have righteousness as their object.
God should rule over all, and everything should be in relation
to him.
Things of the flesh are properly ruled by concupiscence; intellectual things by curiosity; wisdom by pride.
Not that a man cannot boast of riches or knowledge, but that is
not the place for pride; for while granting that a man is learned
it is easy to convince him that he is wrong to be proud.
The proper place for pride is wisdom, for you cannot grant a man
that he has become wise but is wrong to be proud of it, for
it is only right that he should be. Therefore God alone gives
wisdom, and that is why "If a man must boast, let him boast of
the Lord" (1 Corinthians 1:31). (E 721; P 933.)

The irony here is obvious, for Pascal's real point is that a person who is truly wise will put all pride behind him. However,
even in the highest order of valuing the self-centeredness of
the lower orders may appear, in opposition to *charité* itself;
and the only cure for it is the God-centeredness which is given
by grace through humble faith.

The theme of the three orders has frequently been termed
Pascal's most significant contribution to modern thought. Pre-
dictably, it was not admired in the eighteenth century; Voltaire
dismissed the long passage on the subject as "gibberish"; but it
was adapted with many variations in the nineteenth. At all
events, the idea is entirely characteristic and has a kind of cli-
mactic importance for Pascal himself, whatever an individual
reader may decide to make of it. Evidently the theme first took
shape in mathematical inquiry regarding infinity and geometric magnitudes; it grew during Pascal's reflections on human nature; and it was confirmed by his deepened religious
experience. Therefore we are justified in giving prime importance to this view for interpreting his thought and life.

Man, declares Pascal, defines his own world by the sort of
interest he takes in existing, but it is the object of his interest
that makes him the kind of person he is. No man belongs
solely to a single realm of value, although as his life becomes

more and more organized he settles into one order that is increasingly dominant. And yet Pascal goes beyond proposing a typology or analysis of human valuing; he ventures to state an interpretation of the transcendent itself as an acknowledged presence in experience. There is a right way of ordering the orders, and it is made visible only to the eyes of faith in God.[42]

III

And so the time has come for discussing Pascal's thought of God. If the task is approached with some hesitation, this may be partly due to a warning given in the *Pensées:*

> A workman who talks about wealth, a lawyer who talks about war, about kingship, etc. But the rich man rightly speaks of wealth, the king speaks casually of a great gift he has just made, and God rightly speaks of God. (E 580; P 303.)

Obviously, one should speak only about what he knows, for competence alone inspires credibility. If this is true in human matters, it is doubly true with respect to God. This means that unless God chooses to make himself known he cannot be known at all. The initiative lies with him. Our comprehension of God depends upon a communication from God. In short, Pascal expresses here, in an arresting way, his belief in *revelation*. It is impossible, he holds, that God should ever be the end if he is not the beginning too.

Again, a lower order cannot generate a higher order out of itself. Pascal was not, and had no reason to be, an evolutionary thinker. He had learned as a mathematician that a line is not produced by accumulating points, nor a surface by accumulating lines, nor a solid by accumulating surfaces. As a Christian he is likewise convinced that man's knowledge of God cannot be the mere projection of human experience, even to infinity. Such knowledge, if it is possible, must be due to God's disclosing himself to man.

This means that Pascal is decidedly skeptical of any effort to prove God by the works of nature, as Saint Thomas had

believed possible and many of Pascal's contemporaries such as
Grotius and Fénelon still held. He is equally convinced that
God cannot be reached as the conclusion of a rational argument, like Q.E.D. in geometry. God is to be known on his
terms, not on man's. Pascal believes in revelation as emphati-
cally as does any thinker of the Protestant Reformation, but
his belief is basically Catholic in stressing the priority, rather
than the sole authority, of revelation. In other words, the view
of the transcendent, infinite God which Pascal holds is one that
is inclusive, not exclusive. The highest order is not out of all
relation to the lower orders but sets them in relation. All the
orders, however distinct and distant when seen from below,
converge at infinity, which is to say in God, when seen by faith
from above. And it is this ordering convergence which gives
each separate order its place and rightness in the whole of
things. Just as the exercise of intelligence involves no abroga-
tion of physical fact or material power, so the opening of the
heart to _charité_ is the fulfillment and not the annihilation of
the mind's search for the truth. The infinite includes the finite
as the finite cannot possibly include the infinite. Perhaps it is
fortunate that Pascal never separated his view of God from
that of infinity which mathematical inquiry opened up to him.
This close association in his mind may have been instrumental
in fashioning an approach to God that breathes a spirit of personal discovery and venture rather than that of literal, dogmatic finality.

"I marvel at the audacity with which these people go around
speaking of God," Pascal declares. (E 49; P 781.) He is evidently thinking of those philosophers and theologians who try
to prove God's existence by nature and reason alone. Pascal's
outburst may seem puzzling at first, since he plainly believes
that logical argument based on visible phenomena is the model
of human knowledge. However, it is out of order when one is
speaking of God. The heart of God has its own reasons which
human reasoning cannot know. Therefore Pascal expresses his
amazement at the rashness of relying solely on demonstrative
proof where the order of _charité_ is concerned. How can anyone

claim to know so much? Those who already believe in God have no need of such proof, since they see tokens of God's presence and power wherever they look in the universe. And those who do not believe, at least not yet, will never come to faith merely because such proof is offered; the knowledge of God must always proceed from the love of God. A certain modesty and even skepticism is appropriate to faith, which is the cause and not the effect of any genuine understanding of God.

This brings us to a consideration of the theme of the *hidden* God, which figures prominently in the latter half of the *Pensées*. The idea is a complex one and serves more than one purpose in Pascal's defense of Christianity. Hence it has been interpreted in many contradictory ways by students of Pascalian thought. This theme of the *Dieu caché* can probably be traced in part to Pascal's long-delayed conversion, which must have seemed an answer to the prayer he shared with the psalmist, "Oh that I knew where I might find him!" It would also have been reinforced by his thoughtful reading of the Scriptures, giving confirmation to Pascal's view that only God speaks rightly of God.

Quoting from the Vulgate (Isa. 45:15), *"Vere tu es Deus absconditus,"* he translates the verse sometimes simply as *Dieu caché* but prefers the longer expressions of his own, "A God who hides himself" and "A God who chooses to hide himself." The change from passive participle to active present tense is highly significant. Pascal is saying that God retains control over his own self-revealing so that there is both clarity and obscurity in the act of revelation itself. And it is not as if all the obscurity were on man's side and all the clarity on God's. Dialectically and rather paradoxically, Pascal uses the theme of God's hiddenness precisely to protect and guard the divine initiative in revelation.

At the risk of overemphasis, Pascal insists that the God who verily hides himself is the same God who reveals himself, and that he reveals himself as the hidden God. This in his view is not because God plays games with man or takes sadistic delight in mystifying man, but because God wills to *be* God in his speech and action toward man. Thus when Moses asked for the name of the mysterious one who addressed him out of the bush that burned without being consumed, he received the cryptic answer, "I AM WHO I AM" (Ex. 3:14). Pascal's own night of fire had brought to him a similar sense that God *is,* just because he is unwilling to be pinned down in man-made definitions, expectations, or requirements.

But Pascal carries the theme farther. One of his ablest interpreters, Henri Gouhier, gives the fullest, most illuminating account of its reverberations and implications.[43] The *Dieu caché* is not only what might be termed a theological protective device; it is a major motif leading into Pascal's whole vision of the world under God. Gouhier correctly regards as the basic text the letter to Charlotte de Roannez in which Pascal makes the following declaration:

> Ordinarily God hides himself, and discloses himself rarely to those whom he wishes to engage in his service. . . . All things cover up some mystery; all things are the veils that cover God. Christians ought to recognize him in everything.[44]

This has the force of a general principle for Pascal, applicable to many matters of faith. If God always concealed himself, the letter goes on, there would not be any merit in believing; and if he never concealed himself, there would of course be very little faith at all. The rare occasions of God's self-disclosure— such as the miracle of the Holy Thorn which is the immediate cause of this letter—both encourage and limit faith. No one should expect of Christianity something it does not pretend to give, namely a nonmysterious understanding of God. For faith itself, God is hidden in the works of nature, where nevertheless some pagans have known how to recognize him (Rom. 1:20); he is hidden in the Bible, where the Jews discovered his will in the Law and the Prophets while pagans could not; he is hidden even in the incarnation where he "covers himself with

humanity"; and he is hidden in the Eucharist, "the most obscure and strange secret of all," under the species of his real
presence in the bread and wine.

Thus by a typical Pascalian *tour de force* a principle apparently designed to protect God from the prying eyes of reason
becomes instead a rule for understanding everything in terms
of God. For if all things mask God, then all things speak of
God, though not directly or positively. His very absence becomes a strange kind of presence, possibly the most unmistakable kind of all; and his silence, although it may cause pain in
a believer's heart, speaks far more loudly than any human
speech about him.

In the *Pensées* this fundamental theme recurs in dialogue
with the nonbeliever:

> Instead of complaining that God has hidden himself, you will
> thank him for having revealed so much of himself; and you will
> thank him too for not having revealed himself to the proud
> *savants* who are unworthy to know a God so holy. . . . There is
> enough light for those who wish only to see, and enough darkness
> for those who are contrary-minded. (E 310, 309; P 394, 149.)

Here the thought is introduced that God's hiddenness, while
due primarily to the divine will itself, is also secondarily due
to man's contrary-mindedness. No one can see God who refuses to look, or who will not read the ambiguous signs of
nature and history aright. This thought is rendered with many
variations. It occurs in the Provincial Letters in several contexts such as the treatment of Christ's presence as "real though
veiled" (the sixteenth Letter) and that of the truth of Christianity in the face of the multiplicity of sects and religions (the
seventeenth Letter).

The same thought reappears in numerous fragments destined for the Apology where Pascal adapts to his purpose
Biblical passages that speak of God blinding men's eyes, making their ears deaf, hardening their hearts, or throwing a veil
over the truth. The Messiah who came was not the Messiah
whom the Jews had expected; nothing could better ensure that

seeing they should not see, and hearing they should not hear. Miracles and prophecies (even when fulfilled) produce disbelief as well as belief. The word of God to Isaiah telling him to make his people blind is commented upon by the four Evangelists and Saint Paul (Isa. 6:9–10; Matt. 13:14; Mark 4:12; Luke 8:10; John 12:39–41; Rom. 10:8); the Old Testament passage is used to explain Jewish resistance to Jesus reported in the New. Thus Pascal asserts: "One understands nothing of the works of God unless he starts from the principle that God willed to blind some and enlighten others." (E 439; P 232.)

Therefore the motif of the *Dieu caché* is closely linked in Pascal's mind with the doctrine of election or predestination: "There is enough clarity to enlighten the elect, and enough obscurity to humble them. There is enough obscurity to blind the reprobate, and enough clarity to condemn them and leave them without excuse." (E 443; P 236.) But if God blinds some persons to the signs and wonders of his presence, how can they be held responsible for not seeing them? Pascal attempts to maintain the real ambiguity or equivocation in God's dealings with men while at the same time affirming that this ambiguity is relative to human refusal or acceptance of salvation. He thus finds himself caught in the same contradiction that plagues all hard-line predestinarian thinking, but makes a strenuous effort to soften it. Without abandoning his belief that human wills are finally willed by God, Pascal nevertheless holds that God gives some persons the grace to seek him with all their hearts, and this indicates that they are capable of finding God who though unknown is not absolutely unknowable. Salvation, though finally the gift of God to men, is not an open-or-shut case, a *fait accompli*, for God has established the possibility of faith in him by virtue of the very mystery and ambiguity of human existence itself.[45]

Pascal's conception of God, then, follows the lines of Pauline and Augustinian rather than strictly Jansenist interpretation. God in his hiddenness signifies not sheer incomprehensibility or arbitrariness, but that "deep but dazzling darkness" of which Henry Vaughan wrote. It is this hiddenness which makes

everything comprehensible at last to faith. All our seeing must
be done "in a glass, darkly" as Saint Paul confessed; yet this
avowal of partial ignorance and obscurity makes faith both
necessary and possible. For Pascal, too, the discovery of a Dieu
caché rebuffs man's ingrained *libido sciendi* while at the same
time calling forth his will to believe.[46]

For Pascal, God's hiddenness manifests his Godhood as seen
darkly but dazzlingly by the eyes of faith. This view is that
found in the Jewish Scriptures reinterpreted by Christian doctrine. It directs attention to the Transcendent: the action of
the eternal in and through the temporal, the spirit "figured"
in the letter, infinity made visible to human finitude. Pascal
believes that transcendence is a horizon or dimension of man's
own experience, for he writes:

> The God of the Christians is a God who makes the soul feel
> that in him alone can it find peace; that only in loving him can
> it find joy; and who at the same time makes it loathe the
> obstacles which hold it back and prevent it from loving God
> with all its might. . . . This God makes the soul aware of the
> underlying self-love which is destroying it, and which alone he
> can cure. (E 302; P 460.)

IV

The Jesuit-Jansenist controversy in which Pascal played a
leading role can be described in differing ways. It had a political aspect, evident in the suspicion and hostility with which
Richelieu, Mazarin, and Louis XIV regarded the stubborn
nonconformity of Port-Royal when attacked by the ecclesiastical authorities. But the controversy was far more than a power
struggle between opposing factions in French Catholicism;
basically, it represented two perennial and antithetical tendencies within Christian history as a whole, which Jean Mesnard
calls the Roman sense of order and the spiritual ferment of the
Gospels.[47]

At the heart of this controversy lay a profound and much-
debated theological issue of extreme importance to Pascal him-

self. It had to do with the relationship between divine grace and human free will. In 1588 the Spanish Jesuit Molina had published a work on *The Harmony of Free Will with the Gifts of Grace*. He took the position that God gives to fallen man, sinful though he is, the "sufficient grace" enabling him to will and work for his salvation. It is therefore man's will that makes God's "sufficient" grace truly "efficacious" by a kind of simultaneous cooperation.

This book occasioned much protest from Augustinian and Thomistic quarters, as it seemed to deny predestination by making man responsible for his own salvation. The most influential opposition to Molinism was aroused by a book called *Augustinus,* written by Cornelius Jansen, a Flemish professor of theology and bishop whose ideas had been conveyed to France primarily by Saint-Cyran, imprisoned by Richelieu as one step in the persecution of Port-Royal with which Saint-Cyran had been closely associated. The *Augustinus* was conceived as a massive defense of Augustinian doctrine to the detriment of the Pelagian heresy combated by the "doctor of grace" over a thousand years before, and which the followers of Jansen found anew in Molinism. Jansen himself held that in man's original condition, symbolized by Adam, the will was indeed free yet drawn toward God; but after the Fall, man was entirely moved by self-love and so has no real freedom any longer. This condition can be changed only by "the grace of Jesus Christ" which liberates man's will for the love of God instead of self. The Molinist idea that man can still choose whether to be saved or not is therefore opposed by the Augustinian idea that only God's grace can liberate man from his so-called freedom which is really bondage. Willing and loving are identical, determined by the object of attraction; grace, when it comes, makes God rather than self the *delectatio victrix,* or victorious delight, which is interior and irresistible.

To be sure, Jansen's Augustinianism is presented with a kind of ecstatic severity quite foreign to Augustine himself, except in some extreme passages written in the heat of anti-Pelagian controversy. The Jesuit critics of Jansenist theology detected, quite understandably, similarities with Lutheran and Calvinist doctrines. Pascal and the Port-Royalists defended Jansenism against such charges, but Pascal's concern in the *Provincial Letters* is not only controversial; he wishes to make clear how the grace of God operates with regard to human sin and salvation. In short, he becomes increasingly involved in theological issues as such, of course agreeing fundamentally with the Jansenist interpretation, yet gaining confidence and a measure of independence as he proceeds.

With the fourth Letter, published on February 25, 1656, the doctrine of grace comes into special prominence. In the first three Letters, Pascal has been sighting the Jesuit target and building up popular sympathy for his own cause. The fourth, however, marks a change of strategy. To defend Antoine Arnauld has now become useless as the Sorbonne censure has gone through as expected, so Pascal moves toward a direct attack. Underneath the badinage there is an earnestness that cannot possibly be missed. What is at stake in this conflict, according to Pascal, is God's right to be God instead of merely a religious object or resource. Grace means the good will of God toward men, not the accompaniment or complement of human will and action. Grace is "prevenient," in the language of theology—it comes before and does not follow upon man's intention or effort. It is truly "sovereign" in that it cannot be guaranteed or manipulated by any work of man, however good.

This fourth Letter includes an imaginary conversation with a Jesuit regarding what his order teaches about divine grace. The father solemnly informs his visitor that "an action cannot be imputed as a sin unless God bestows on us, before committing it, the knowledge of the evil that is in the action and an inspiration which moves us to avoid it." [48] Hence an action is not sinful unless it is deliberate and avoidable; to sin at all implies the ability not to sin, and this ability is provided by knowing in advance the evil consequences of the possible act and by a countering motive inspiring its avoidance. The knowledge and the inspiration together constitute what the Jesuits, following Molina, term "actual grace." To this Pascal retorts in effect that such a view makes a mortal sin so hard to commit that it becomes one of the most difficult things in the world to be damned.

His refutation is precise and pitiless: If the sinfulness of my act depends upon my attention being called in advance to the avoidable evil it entails, then the less I think about escaping evil the more I secure myself against falling into it. The Jesuit's visitor exclaims:

> Oh Father, what a blessing this will be for some people I know! I must certainly introduce them to you. Probably you have never met with people who had fewer sins. For in the first place, they never think of God at all; their vices have got the better of their reason; they have never known either their weakness or the doctor who is capable of curing them. . . . What a fine way to be happy in this world and the next! . . . None of your half-and-half sinners, who at least retain some love of virtue; they will be damned every one, these semi-sinners. But as for those open sinners, hardened sinners, unmixed, full, and accomplished sinners, hell cannot hold them; they have cheated the devil just by abandoning themselves to him! [49]

This Jesuit theory is contradicted by the fact that there are thousands of people "who have no such desires, who sin without regret, who even boast of sinning." We do not habitually feel remorse *before* committing sinful acts. Sin is not always conscious of itself, even prospectively. There can be, and there are, sins of ignorance and of surprise. These are the human facts and no Christian teaching should go contrary to them.

Pascal's imaginary Jansenist now tries to bring logic and Scripture to bear upon the issue. True, he says, an action can be worthy of blame only if it is a voluntary one, but this does not mean that the actor must have previewed the good or evil in it. Saint Augustine and Aristotle are agreed on this and the Bible gives numerous examples. The question then becomes, What does "voluntary" mean? Clearly, it means freedom of action and therefore of will; otherwise one could not justly be held accountable for sin.

But what, again, does freedom mean? What indeed, if not

self-determination, "being myself"? Whereas the Molinists held
that a person is what he does, the Jansenists—Augustinians as
they were—declared that a person does what he is. The roots of
sin therefore lie deeper down than one's conscious intention or
ability. We do what we do because of what we are—sinful
through and through, as the myth of the Fall makes clear.
Concupiscence has usurped *charité* as the moving power of the,
will. Man's God-given freedom has in fact become unfree; even
his conscience has been darkened and weakened, so that he has
no built-in monitor to guide or protect him from sin.

Pascal shares the Augustinian view of man's original, radical sinfulness. What he writes about unconscious or inadvert-
ent sin is not simply the sad judgment of a man who has been
around in the world, keenly noting human frailties and failures. It springs, rather, from the conviction stated by Arnauld
and Jansen, and by the ancient fathers and Saint Paul, that
unless a human act is motivated by the love of God it can be
neither right nor good. Therefore it is only in the light of
grace that we know sin to *be* sin, just as only in the light of
sin do we know grace to *be* grace.

Sin and grace presuppose one another, logically and theologically. Realizing this, Pascal treats the relationship dialectically, almost contrapuntally; he understands it as a profoundly
mysterious involvement in which we have to do with God,
whether we will and know it or not, and God has to do with
us, whether we deserve and desire it or not. In the fourth
Provinciale, where the issue is that of human responsibility,
Pascal accepts Augustine's view that human nature is corrupt,
but rejects Jansen's position that there can be personal guilt
without responsibility. At the same time Pascal refuses the
Jesuit idea that sin can be identified with single, conscious, voluntary actions, because he is aware that its roots lie deeper
down in the subsoil of personal selfhood itself. Grace, then,
means God's mercy to the sinner despite his sin, yet also because of his sin; we are indeed held responsible for some things
we cannot help doing in our fallen state, but God tempers justice with mercy to forgive us our sin.

THE BELIEVER133

Pascal's case against the Jesuits would certainly have been stronger if he had not, in the later *Letters,* so easily associated sin with gambling, dueling, oaths, Mardi Gras misbehavior, and the like. It is basic to his whole perspective that sin should not be understood in such an atomistic and fragmented way. Nevertheless his argument is Augustinian, even if his illustrations have a Jansenist or Puritan ring to them.

Pascal's divergence from hard-line Jansenism comes out more clearly in the *Pensées* than it does in the *Provinciales.* Arnauld and Jansen had sharply distinguished grace from nature, but Pascal writes:

> Grace will always be in the world, and so will nature, so that grace is in some way natural. (E 765; P 662.)

While nature and grace are not to be confused, since they belong to different orders, it is still true that grace permeates and transforms nature—especially human nature—in such a way that "man infinitely surpasses man" by virtue of the grace which beckons and enables him. The infinite distance seen from below is resolved in principle by a continuity ordered from above. As Jacques Chevalier puts it:

> We are finite beings suspended from the Infinite and tending towards it with all our powers. The magnetic pole for humanity is God. There is nothing that can ever take the place of God for the human being. . . . God alone can satisfy the demands of both reason and the heart, because he alone is our true good and he alone is worthy of our love.[50]

Another example of Pascal's independent thinking on grace is this:

> The least movement affects the whole of nature; the entire sea changes because of a rock. So also, in the realm of grace, the least action affects everything by its results. Therefore everything is important. (E 749; P 927.)

This is an instance of that view of transcendence as including all things, which we noted earlier in speaking of God. It is only an analogy, of course, but its importance lies in expressing Pascal's often repeated conviction that visible things truly represent the invisible, being the sensible image of what is spiritual, so that nature becomes an image of grace. Furthermore, the Pascalian idea places him within a far ampler tradition of Christian thought than his Jansenist influences would suggest. Here he echoes the Neoplatonic side of Augustine and the earlier church fathers, where the same symbolic and relational understanding of grace is expressed.

Pascal's own way of thinking about grace is also unmistakably shown in his *Ecrits sur la Grâce,* probably begun before the time of the *Provinciales* and the *Pensées.*[51] The main point to be noticed is that Pascal's statement is a balanced one avoiding doctrinaire extremes and oversimplifications altogether. He understands that the choice is not *between* grace and freedom, as both must be affirmed on the basis of Christian experience. The real question to be answered is "whether the will of man is the cause of the will of God, or the will of God is the cause of the will of man"; Pascal has no doubt that the latter is true. He finds in Scripture many passages showing that

> when two wills work together to an end while one is the supreme master and infallible cause of the other, then the act can be both attributed and denied to the secondary (or human) will. It can be attributed to the dominant will, and moreover it must not fail to be attributed to it.[52]

For Pascal, God's grace is that "dominant will" which initiates and crowns all human effort. There is then a genuine cooperation of man with God, but not that envisaged by the Molinists in which each single act counts separately and grace is a help or tool to be used in order to gain spiritual success. In common with the Jansenists of Port-Royal, Pascal believes that grace is God's own freedom with which man must always reckon. It is by grace that I am allowed to exist at all and to cooperate with God for my salvation. When I am not caused by grace to do what I should, the fault lies with myself. Yet when I am enabled to do the will of God I do not cease to be myself. Rather, God's grace transforms itself into the motive power of my freedom. Here Pascal's emphasis is different from that of Jansenism, which is typically upon the gratuitousness and not the graciousness of God's grace. A more spacious, classically Christian air breathes through Pascal's own thought regarding the good pleasure of God to offer salvation to all mankind. A word of comfort is to be spoken, though it lies on the other side of a command—the word declared in Christ, "Jesus Christ, the God whom we approach without pride and before whom we humble ourselves without despair" (E 406; P 212).[53]

V

Pascal's thoughts on the meaning of Christ are voiced frequently throughout his later writings. However, they are gathered up and given most luminous expression in his *Mystère de Jésus*, a devotional meditation based on the narrative of Jesus' agony in the garden of Gethsemane as described in Matt., ch. 26. Probably modeled upon a similar meditation by Cornelius Jansen, it appears to have been written for Port-Royal; yet Pascal's work quickly oversteps the limits of an occasional piece and opens up wider ranges of thought with insight and imagination. Although Pascal did not pretend to be original where Christian truth was concerned, this meditation has a freshness and ardent spirituality entirely Pascal's own.

"The true, the truest Pascal is he of the *Mystère de Jésus*," claims Jacques Maritain. What makes this true is the close linking of personal faith and theological lucidity, no strangers to each other in Pascal any more than in Saint Paul, Saint Augustine, or Bonaventura.

The meditation is precisely titled, for Pascal asks the reader to stand with him in the presence of a mystery that may be experienced though not explained. A contrapuntal balance is maintained between Jesus as the "object" of faith whom the believer speaks about, and Jesus as the "subject" who speaks to the believer in his own person. The dialogue form of the whole *Mystère* sustains this tension both aesthetically and theologically. When Jesus is spoken about, the stress is placed on his loneliness, desperation, and vulnerability. But when Jesus speaks, the emphasis shifts at once to the comfort and assurance he brings to the believer.

The very first sentence makes a rather abrupt distinction between the passion and the agony endured by Christ in Gethsemane:

> Jesus suffers in his passion the torments which men inflict upon him; but in his agony he suffers the torments which he inflicts upon himself. . . . This is a suffering from no human but an almighty hand, for he must be almighty to bear it. (E 739; P 919.)[54]

Thus the mystery of the "two natures" of the Christ, his humanity and his divinity, is at once announced. Jesus' passion, caused by sinful men who do not or will not understand his mission, is but the outward expression of his suffering. Its inward and crucial meaning is that of his agony, self-inflicted as the work and will of almighty God. Jesus in the Garden suffers more from God than from men; and it is this fact which marks his oneness with the Father. His agony, brought upon him by his Father, is also self-assumed, for he chooses to be chosen. "He must be almighty to bear it."

Jesus is fully human, however, *vere homo,* grieving, seeking companionship with his disciples, making complaint to God. Nothing in the scene suggests that God is wearing our humanity as a disguise or holding anguished counsel with himself. A human being wrestles with a life-or-death decision, sweating blood "in the horror of the night." Jesus is lonely on earth, left alone to the wrath of God, but he is one with heaven in that loneliness—that is, in knowing why he suffers. In Gethsemane, Jesus is not the pitiful victim of God's power, but the servant of God's purpose, cognizant of the inner necessity and dignity of his suffering.

While there is undoubted mystery in this self-inflicted suffering, this willing self-identification with the will of God, there is a certain propriety as well. Only man can bear the sin of man, yet only God can save man from his sin; and Jesus

Christ is both in his own person. Pascal revitalizes the orthodox doctrine by portraying the very soul of Christ, feeling the
double impact and living at the intersection of two orders,
those of redeeming God and natural man.

The entire "interior colloquy" of the *Mystère* takes place
within this same framework and at the same juncture. The
very sound and rhythm of Pascal's words seem to grow directly
out of his thought regarding Christ. The image and the idea
are one, or as nearly one as human art can make them, in sus-
taining this tension and dynamism. Why does Pascal use
"Jesus" instead of "Christ" throughout his meditation, if not
to accentuate the very lowliness and isolation of God's human-
ness, his humility? Indeed, the lowly agony of Jesus Christ, his
excruciating humanity, is faith's surest sign that God is present
and powerful in him. "Only that which is taken up can be
healed," as Athanasius wrote centuries earlier.

But the clearest indication of Pascal's originality, even
modernity, is to be found in his memorable sentence: "Jesus
will be in agony even to the end of the world; we must not
sleep during all that time." These words have raised theological eyebrows since they were first read. A critic like Henri
Bremond, otherwise favorably disposed toward Pascal, protests
that his is a *Christ diminué;* that for Pascal the world is as
badly off as it was before Christ came; and that Christ has
therefore failed in the mission he was sent by God to accom-
plish. Hence Pascal, Bremond asserts, is here the victim of the
very doubt he struggled ineffectually to overcome, for is he not
saying that Christ has still to win his victory over human sin
and guilt? [55]

Although Bremond's criticism is right in detecting a departure from traditional orthodoxy in this famous sentence, it
misses the mark in several important respects. Pascal's meaning
is not that Christ has yet to do his work as Savior but that the
work of salvation is still being done. In stressing the continuing agony of Christ, Pascal is stressing equally the everlasting
redemption which he offers to mankind. We may be asleep
like his first disciples, but Christ continues to work our salva-

tion even while we know it not. His continuing agony *jusqu'à
la fin du monde* expresses for Pascal the constancy and perpetual availability of Christ as Savior.

Even more important is Pascal's insistence that the work of
Christ is no mere historical happening in calendar time, but a
veritable event in eternity as well. As such it transcends time
by entering and transforming the meaning of chronological
succession and duration. It belongs as much to the human
future as the past, signifying that the time of salvation is
always the Now of alert, decisive faith. This is why Pascal casts
his meditation in the present tense although it refers to a past
event reported in the Bible.

It is not enough to see in the *Mystère* only a reference to
the repetition of Christ's sacrifice in the Mass, for Pascal thinks
of the "real presence" in much wider terms. "I am present
with you through my word in Scripture, through my spirit in
the Church and by inspiration, through my power in the
priests, through my prayer in the faithful." This presence commands the vigilant response of faith. Christ will save us even
though we slumber, since this is God's will for him and for us.
But is it not better to be awake, to know what is going on,
prepared for the appointed end?

Pascal's understanding of faith as an alert and watchful
readiness does not permit God's work in Christ to be taken
for granted: "There is no relation between me and God nor
Jesus Christ the righteous." What he means by this calculated
overstatement is that we are unable to maneuver ourselves into
a righteous position before God just because we believe Christ
died for us. As in his earlier writings on grace, there is no fixed
point of contact, not even "Jesus Christ the righteous," that
stabilizes and secures our salvation so that we can have the last
decisive word regarding it. What we do have, however, is the
assurance, "Console yourself; you would not be seeking me
had you not already found me." Again the Augustinian accent:
the object of the search initiates the search, so that we are not
found by God apart from searching for him, nor simply as a
reward for searching, but in and through the search itself.

What then shall we do to be saved? Pascal's reply is both enigmatic and categorical: "I must add my wounds to his and join myself to him." A strange claim, surely, from the viewpoint of dogmatic certainty in a divine *fait accompli* symbolized by the Son sitting in heaven at the right hand of God the Father. Here Pascal is as modern as Kierkegaard insisting that the believer is contemporaneous with Christ, or as Dietrich Bonhoeffer declaring that "only a suffering God can help." Willingness to suffer now with Christ by participating in his work of suffering love, a readiness that must not be put off till the future, is the touchstone of Christian seriousness and honesty. It is in the members of his body that Christ is in agony until the end of the world, which is to say that his very life lives on in them.

But again the question recurs: Is not Pascal's thought more sensitive to suffering than to victory? May he not therefore be correctly reproached, if not with a *Christ diminué,* then at any rate with a Christ who is presented not so much as the second person of the triune God as "the living solution to man's problem"? [56] That is the opinion of several Catholic critics who have taken the position that Pascal's Christology is turned more toward men than toward God, as it is useful chiefly in order to know man better.

Perhaps it is surprising that the heart of Pascal's faith in Christ has been set forth most plainly by a Jewish thinker, Léon Brunschvicg. Commenting upon this meditation, he wrote:

> It is the very proof or test of the Mediator that he should be abandoned, isolated, even from those between whom he must mediate. Such a proof marks the limit of suffering; the Son of God can scarcely endure it, in the extent to which he has identified himself with the creatures whom his compassion wishes to help. . . . This "unparalleled lament, this extreme sorrow" Pascal composes by the intensity of his meditation, so close to his own humanity that at this moment he is by himself with Jesus. [57]

Whether the *Mystère de Jésus* was intended for Pascal's Apology or not, it is central to his view of Christ in all the later writings. It sets forth poignantly and daringly the power of suffering love to overcome man's natural distance from God. Like the paintings of Grünewald or Rembrandt, the *Mystère* gives striking personal confirmation to the words of the apostle Paul: While there is a sadness that leads to death, there is another sadness that gives life, God's own life, to humble, grateful humanity.

VI

What was the character of Pascal's religious experience, which comes to expression in his thoughts and beliefs concerning God or Christ? The question is important, as it presses for an understanding of Pascal the Christian in terms of what he called the reasons of the heart. However, it is also likely to mislead us if we ask it with the hope of isolating some particular tendency or quality as a comprehensive explanation of his faith. Many accounts are possible, and plausible, but Pascal continues to elude every effort to make him into a Catholic deviate, a Bible-believing crypto-Protestant, an unstable compound of credulity and sophistication, or an advance scout of contemporary existentialism.

In particular, was Pascal a mystic? This question is raised inevitably by the *Mémorial* of his "night of fire" in November, 1654. (E 737; P 913.) It is an authentic, firsthand record of an intensely personal experience that Pascal regarded as evidential and indubitable. God had come out of hiding and had spoken plainly, powerfully to him. The metaphor of fire, familiar in other mystical writings, conveys the feelings both of burning pain and of inner radiance. Biblical resonances are everywhere: quoted fragments, the souvenir of Moses' vision of the burning bush, crosses drawn on the parchment copy. The words "certitude," "joy," "peace" indicate the presence of an unmistakable rapture and assurance. The phrase "Forgetfulness of the world and of everything except God" shows how completely Pascal's energies were engaged and focused by this

experience. If contemplative concentration and ecstatic personal commitment are marks of mysticism, then without doubt
Pascal was a mystic for at least these two hours of his life.

There are other classic mystical traits, however, which Pascal's moving record does not seem to contain. He does not
speak of becoming engulfed or lost in the divine, like Saint
John of the Cross or Saint Theresa. The experience retains the
character of an encounter, of *communion* rather than full
union with God, although the feature of dialogue is not so
pronounced here as in the *Mystère de Jésus*. It is significant
that the words "Grandeur of the human soul" occur in the
Mémorial, rather than terms suggesting that Pascal's personality is being invaded or ravished by a divine overpowering.
And the fact that Pascal is observing himself, taking notes,
even as the "night of fire" occurs, means that he is far from
losing his identity even momentarily in the event itself.

Still more noteworthy is the fact that this unique document
has much to say about *mediated* faith in contrast to the *immediacy* greatly prized by mystics generally. "The ways taught in
the Gospel" must be learned and followed. If the precious
vision is not to fade forever, there is a discipline to be undergone, a spiritual director to be relied on, a whole life of prayer
and charity to be practiced. The *Mémorial* abounds in direc-
tives, resolutions, warnings. Pascal recognizes his creaturely
need for external, even institutional support. He may apply
to himself Saint Paul's words "I know whom I have believed,"
but this does not mean that he will not have to keep on believing where he cannot know. And he prays, twice in the *Mémorial* and once again just before his death, that he may not
be separated from God and Jesus. This expresses his decision
to live henceforth in the clear light of what has happened to
him, not as an individual ecstatic but as a loyal member of the
visible institutional church.

In short, by virtue of a definitely mystical experience, and
by the generally ardent and intense nature of his whole religious life, Pascal has his own place within the tradition of

Christian mysticism. But it is a highly individual place; and one in which the mystical tendencies are offset by others of a more outgoing, practical, rational kind. If he kept close and secret the precious testimony to his two hours with God, it was because he valued the experience for the insight and guidance it could bring to everything else that was to be done, suffered, enjoyed, or understood. He did not, like Meister Eckhart or Saint Theresa, see in rapturous union with God the end of life which left no room for anything else. His "night of fire" marked rather a new beginning, an *approfondissement* and *persévérance* in the order of *charité*.[58]

Another strain native to Pascal's religious life is the ascetic. For all his intellectual brilliance, he had to learn spiritual self-discipline the hard way. Especially during his last years he made strenuous efforts to control his quick temper, pride, and impatience toward those whom he disliked or disdained. The severe atmosphere of Port-Royal in worship (no flowers on the altar, no music in the choir), as well as its almost puritanical strictness and otherworldliness in behavior, probably appealed to Pascal's earnest, often melancholy disposition. Against the advice of his doctors he reduced his living arrangements to the simplest possible terms, would not eat food that pleased him, dismissed his servants, and sheltered sick strangers in his house. He held himself deliberately aloof from family affection, preferring to identify himself with the vagrant poor to whom he gave away most of his income. Sometimes he wore a spiked iron belt next to his skin which he would strike with his fist when distracting thoughts or tempting images assailed him.

The words of Kierkegaard about Pascal's austerities will bear repeating:

> Who has been used so much as Pascal in recent times by pastors and professors? They take his thoughts—but that Pascal was an ascetic, went about with a hair shirt and everything like that— they leave that out. Or they explain it as a birthmark of the period which no longer has any significance for us. Splendid! In all other respects Pascal is original—but not here. But was

asceticism the general thing in his time, then, or had it not
even then been done away with long before, and Pascal was the
one who had to assert it in the face of his time? [59]

We must take Pascal as he was and not as we might prefer to
have him. The ascetic strain in his character is an unavoidable
fact. Although a fixed penitential posture must have been very
difficult for him to maintain, he made repeated efforts to adopt
it. Believing that "the external must be joined to the internal"
in religion, he limped painfully from his rooms to Saint-Sulpice
and back almost daily, whenever he was able, to attend Mass.
He gave alms personally, lavishly, to the poor people he met
by chance, confessing that he loved poverty because Jesus loved
it, and adding:

> I love wealth because it gives me the means of helping the un-
> fortunate. I keep faith with everyone. I do not return evil to
> those who do evil to me but wish them a condition like my
> own, in which neither good nor evil is suffered at the hands of
> men. I try to be just, genuine, sincere, and loyal to all. . . . These
> are my feelings; and every day of my life I bless my Redeemer
> who implanted them in me, and who has turned a man full of
> weaknesses, miseries, lust, pride, and ambition into one free from
> all these failings by the power of his grace. (E 748, P 931.)

Therefore Pascal's religiousness was no mere private affair
between himself and his God; it had both a sacramental base
and a social outreach. It has been said that there was something sturdy and wholesome even in his excesses, for he had
discovered that to do his Christian duty brought a real delight.
So he writes: "The Christian hope of possessing an infinite
good is combined with real enjoyment as well as with fear."
One should not underestimate the strength of pleasurable
emotions in Pascal's sense of the divine. But they are kept in
check, as we might expect, by that element of holy fear which
figures prominently in Jansenist devotional writings. Pascal
distinguishes clearly between false fear of God arising from
doubt and true fear coming from faith. Some persons are

afraid to lose God, while some are actually afraid to find him. This *pensée* best expresses his judgment:

> Somebody told me once that when he came from confession he felt great joy and confidence. Another told me that he was still fearful. At which I thought that these two together would make one good man, and that each was lacking in being without the feeling of the other. (E 747, 757; P 917, 712.)

This same habit of mind, discriminating yet inclusive, informs Pascal's writing on most subjects. His religious sensibility, in particular, expresses his guiding belief that the mark of human greatness is humility before that which is more than human. Thus a perspective is established for the right ordering of all experience, religion included. It is sometimes said that Pascal made religion central and controlling in his life and thought, but this can be confusing if it is taken to suggest that he equated religious obligation and observance with the order of *charité* itself.

Spokesmen for Catholicism have often questioned Pascal's orthodoxy and even his loyalty. It is true that he had ambivalent feelings toward the papacy, insisting that a pope could err in matters of fact and observing that France was perhaps the only country where one could say that the Council is above the Pope. However, these were Gallican views shared by many other Catholics whose regard for the papal office was not open to doubt. "Kings dispose of their kingdoms, but popes cannot dispose of theirs." (E 851; P 708.)

The church, for Pascal, is "a body composed of thinking members; . . . to be a member is to have life, being, and movement only through the spirit of the body and for the sake of the body" (E 688; P 372). That is about as organic and integral a conception of church membership as the most convinced religious institutionalist could expect. At the same time it is far removed from any merely organizational conformity enforced by worldly sanctions and authorities. Instead of the Jesuit word "obedience" Pascal used the more personal spiritual word "submission" to signify that his discipleship to

Jesus Christ was what mattered supremely to him. It was of
Christ that he wrote:

> For by virtue of his glory as God he is all that is great, and by
> virtue of his mortal life he is all that is poor and wretched.
> His purpose in assuming this unhappy state was to enable him-
> self to be present in all persons and the model for all conditions
> of mankind. (E 741; P 946.)

5. The Artist

Friedrich Nietzsche once announced: "There are posthumous men—myself, for example." This could also have been said of Blaise Pascal. There is a book by Bernard Amoudru, titled *La Vie Posthume des Pensées,* which surveys the changing fortunes of Pascal's best-known work throughout three hundred years, showing how it has fascinated readers in every century, attracting some and repelling others, while being reinterpreted by scholars and critics in various and conflicting ways.

It is not easy to maintain neutrality where Pascal is concerned, since he addresses his reader *au fond du coeur* and seems to be pressing for an answer. Extravagant praise and violent antipathy have been aroused and given expression. Rather often Pascal appears to divide the reader against himself, eliciting both positive and negative responses which make objective judgment difficult. This in itself is a tribute to Pascal's exceptional ability to arouse and engage his readers, and on that point there has been little disagreement over the past three centuries. While estimates of his achievement in science, human understanding, and religious philosophy have always differed, his stature as a writer is universally acknowledged.

Nevertheless, one is led to wonder if Pascal would have enjoyed his literary success. He might have been puzzled that his style should have been praised by those whom he failed to convince. A lifelong student and admirer of the *Pensées,* Zacharie

Tourneur, concluded that they contain a rough draft of what was perhaps an embryonic philosophical novel. His verdict was that it would be a serious mistake to consider the liveliness and *agrément* of the *Pensées* as indicative of their truth. Did not Pascal himself, asked Tourneur, regard truth and beauty as distinct, even opposed standards of human achievement? [60]

No, this was not Pascal's view, as one of his *pensées* on eloquence proves. He writes that eloquence requires both the agreeable and the true, "but the agreeable must itself be taken from the true" (E 958; P 667). The beauties of his style have received far more attention than Pascal himself would have wished, to the neglect of the substantive claims which he intended to put before his readers.

Be that as it may, Pascal's art as a writer is part and parcel of his thought, a salient feature of his total work. Style is always finally inseparable from content, and never more so than in the case of Pascal; but this does not forbid, rather it encourages, an attentive regard to the manner in which Pascal reaches and holds his readers.

I

The Art of Persuading

One does not listen to a sermon, says Pascal, in the same way one hears vespers. Since the language of exhortation and of worship is different, the response should also be different. Pascal's own use of language is amazingly diverse and elastic, calling for a whole spectrum of responses. Moreover, he is a conscious craftsman in search of a rule or principle for communicating truth through language. Over forty of the *Pensées* are devoted to this subject alone. Although he might have preferred to let his work speak for itself, what he actually left behind him is an over-the-shoulder acquaintance with the man himself at work, which means that his purposes and processes as a writer are exposed to a rare degree. Thus, while Pascal might have been indignant at being called a man of letters,[61] his readers know that he was one nevertheless.

The problem of communication took a very personal form for him. His sister Gilberte spoke with surprising frankness of Pascal's tendency to dominate any conversation in which he took part. At the same time he was a born persuader whose aggressiveness was held in check by a high regard for truth coming from any quarter. Moreover, he was certainly not lacking in compassion or sympathy for his fellow human beings. He was able to think and write from a viewpoint not his own, so effectively that he could momentarily become the skeptic, atheist, or rationalist whose position he was actually combating. All his life he was an eager conversationalist who carried on his search for truth by means of dialogue with others, and this trait is evident in his writing.

Set off by keen curiosity, indignation, or impassioned conviction, Pascal worked to shape a lucid insight into words. His unusual gift for joining verbal precision with suggestive feeling describes, if it does not entirely explain, the singular force of much that he wrote. He did not think first and write afterward but used his writing to correct and complete his thought. The handwritten text of the *Pensées* shows both the breathless pace at which he worked and the almost endless alterations made as he proceeded. We are told that some of the *Provincial Letters* were redrafted ten or fifteen times.

As always, Pascal was searching for a general rule or principle to be followed in his writing. How is one person able to win the assent of another? The essay *L'Art de Persuader* gives Pascal's answer. "Everyone knows," he declares, "that there are two *entrées* through which opinions are received in the soul, which are its two chief faculties, the understanding and the will." He goes on:

> The more natural is that of the understanding, for one ought never to consent except to demonstrated truths; but the more usual, although against nature, is that of the will, for almost all men are led to believe not by proof, but by *agrément*. This way is low, unworthy, and irrelevant, and also everyone disowns it.[62]

As the mind is moved by generally known truths, so the will is moved by generally shared desires. Ideally, of course, we should assent only to that which follows logically from common principles and obvious facts. In fact, however, our wills are most often influenced by whatever has "a close agreement with the objects of our satisfaction," and therefore the persuader's art must consist in bringing about this agreement. This art, Pascal says, is "incomparably more difficult, more subtle, more useful, and more admirable" than that of rational proof, despite the fact that it is "lower" and less "natural."

This is true, he points out with reluctant realism, even in the scientific field. A proof or demonstration in science is no mere accumulation of data; the form, or "elegance," in which the data are presented is what makes them finally persuasive. This is not because the scientist as such, even if he exists "as such," is in the business of winning friends and influencing people. But he does want his discoveries or observations to be believed in for the sake of scientific progress itself. Pascal is quite aware that it is possible to come up with a dispassionate argument which for all its purely demonstrative finality on paper cannot bring any change in the attitudes, motives, or habits of the person who says he accepts the proof. Real persuasion, then, distinct from scientific demonstration, must consist in an artful mingling of both the *esprit géométrique* and the *esprit de finesse*. Each must subtly reinforce and complement the other if genuine persuasion is to result.

What Pascal wishes to effect in his writing, then, is a correspondence or rapport between the need or readiness of his reader and the proposal that is being made to him. "There is a certain model of *agrément* and beauty between our nature, weak or strong as it is, and whatever pleases us." (E 931; P 585.) Since we are made in order to think and yet subject to deceiving powers, that which pleases us must take account of our capacity for truth while recognizing our liability to error as well. Pascal's art of persuasion embodies his sense of man's dignity and frailty, taken together.

Clearly Pascal is on the tract of a significant idea, characteristically dialectical and ironic, in saying that a kind of combat or "dubious balance . . . between verity and voluptuousness" must be reckoned with in the persuader's art. But having observed that to convince is not the same as to please, "for men are ruled so much more by caprice than by reason," he then proceeds to safer ground and lays down principles only for definitions, axioms, and demonstrations in *L'Art de Persuader*. Although he realizes that conviction and persuasion are indeed different, persuasion must include an element of conviction. He would have approved Léon Bloy's advice: "Always aim at the head, to be sure of hitting no lower than the heart."

Another principle which Pascal seeks to follow in his writing is that of complete naturalness. "Eloquence is a painting of thought, and so those who having painted add still more, make a tableau instead of a portrait." (E 955; P 578.) Painters such as Philippe de Champaigne and Nicolas Poussin, Pascal's contemporaries, believed that art is the imitation of nature. Eloquence is similar to painting in being the honest, transparent expression of an original object—in this case, a thought— and any further embellishment or elaboration, as Pascal says, is to violate nature by masking and disguising it. There are times when one ought to call Paris simply "Paris" and other times when it should be called "the capital of the kingdom." Pascal had no use for the burlesque or the *précieuse* vogue in writing, admired by some in his period. His own preference is for plain statement, common and familiar terms, simple sentences, direct address. He concludes his essay on the art of persuading by saying, "I hate these blown-up words."

Gilberte's biography adds a valuable testimony to her brother's own statements:

> He regarded eloquence as a way of saying things so that all to whom one spoke could understand easily and pleasurably; and he believed that the art consisted in certain dispositions found between the mind and the heart of those spoken to. . . . That is why he studied the heart of man so carefully, as well as his mind. . . . When he thought of something, he put himself in the place of those who should understand it. . . . Finally, he

was such a master of his style that he said everything he wished
to say and what he said always had the effect he intended.[63]

Pascal, then, was a principled writer who knew what he was
doing and why. Where he writes "natural" we would ordinarily write "human" today; he based his art of persuasion upon
his long, careful study of man. His principles are classical,
echoing Ovid's *Ars Poetica* and the rhetoric of Seneca, rather
than that of Cicero, whose more sedate and formal style did
not appeal to him. He knows that "naturalness" in writing
does not come naturally but demands considerable art and
self-discipline.

Pascal makes no effort to improve upon the rules laid down
by grammarians and rhetoricians in his century for effective
speaking and writing. He does, however, enunciate familiar
principles with a vigor and freshness that evoke Montaigne, to
whom he was conspicuously indebted:

> *Style.* When we come across a natural style we are astonished and
> delighted, for we expected to see an author and we find a man.
> Persons of good taste, on the contrary, who see a book and
> expect to find a man, are surprised at finding an author. . . .
>
> When a natural discourse depicts a passion or an effect, one feels
> within oneself the truth of what is heard, which was there all
> the time without his knowing it. Hence one is likely to love a
> man who enables him to feel it, for he has shown us something
> not of his richness, but our own.
>
> Nature diversifies and imitates. Art imitates and diversifies. (E 3,
> 957, 953; P 675, 652, 541.)

Writing according to nature, however, does not mean merely
following the rules, for Pascal any more than for Montaigne.
Thus, although he does not seek novelty for its own sake, Pascal can make a spirited defense of his originality:

> Let nobody say that I have said nothing new; the arrangement
> of the material is new. When playing tennis, we both use the
> same ball, but one of us places it better. . . . As if the same
> thoughts, arranged differently, did not form another body of

> language—so too, the same words differently arranged form new thoughts! (E 4; P 696.)

Since he is trying to adopt a natural style proportioned to the needs and wants of real persons, Pascal knows that he must discover and employ whatever openings he can:

> Inconstancy. We think we are playing an ordinary organ when we deal with men. True, man is an organ, but a strange, unstable, variable organ. . . . Those who can play only the standard organ will not feel at home with this one. You have to know where the stops are. (E 103; P 55.)

Rules for writing may only be forgotten when they have been learned, but they are made to be broken when the human situation requires it. As Pascal says, *la vraie éloquence se moque de l'éloquence,* just as a true morality makes light of morality (E 911; P 513). In a judicious summing up of Pascal's own style, Morris W. Croll has written:

> Pascal is usually spoken of as a "classical" writer; but the term means nothing as applied to him except that he is a writer of tried artistic soundness. He is, in fact, as modernistic, as bold a breaker of the rules and forms of rhetoric, as his master Montaigne, though he is also a much more careful artist.[64]

The correctness of this judgment will be confirmed by looking more closely at the craftsmanship of Pascal's "little letters" and the *pensées* which were destined for his Apology, notably the one called "The Wager."

II

The Provincial Letters

In choosing the letter form for his defense of Antoine Arnauld against the Jesuits of the Sorbonne, Pascal adopted a device that had already become popular among frequenters of salons and the Court. These anonymous missives tended to be on the frothy, frivolous side, relaying juicy gossip, paying well-turned compliments, furthering someone's social ambitions. Pascal took this form and filled it with a new, serious kind of content. His *petites Lettres* therefore exemplify his double-barreled principle that the pleasing should serve as the vehicle of the true.

The other form embodied in the *Provinciales* is that of a pamphlet: a brief, unbound essay on a subject of current interest, likely to be marked by indignation and invective. Pamphleteering had become extremely popular, especially in England, in connection with religious and political controversy during the sixteenth and seventeenth centuries. In France the earliest pamphlets were chiefly given to satire and polemics, such as the *mazarinades* named for the cardinal against whom they were directed. These leaflets were seldom distinguished for either taste or talent, but they were in great demand and enjoyed a wide if transient fame. Usually they were written anonymously and printed in secret, then peddled on the Pont-Neuf or in the most frequented taverns. Although "pamphlet" and "pamphleteer" were terms of disdain in most literary circles, it will be recalled that Milton and Swift in England, or Pascal and Voltaire in France, adapted this form to their purposes, giving it a high degree of excellence and even permanence.

Pascal's letter-pamphlets may be conveniently divided into two parts. The first ten, written "to a friend in the provinces," deal with the censure of Arnauld in the Sorbonne before and after it occurred. They possess a verve and gusto noticeably lacking in the letters Pascal wrote over his own name—nonchalant bantering, casual asides, conversational rhythms abound. Excerpts from Jesuit treatises, culled by Pascal's fellow controversialists at Port-Royal, are sandwiched in between witty sallies and astonished exclamations. For one who professed such distaste for the theater, Pascal's dramatic instinct as he sets the stage, introduces characters, and personifies issues is amazingly sure and fertile.

Trained in the dry, precise language of science, and personally favoring the style appropriate to definition and demonstration, Pascal found a new *métier* in the first ten *Provinciales*. His success is all the more noteworthy since it depends upon a carefully wrought illusion, a contrived authenticity. Substantive issues are always present—the sufficient grace that does not suffice, the difference between *fait* and *droit,* the theory and practice of casuistry—but this is not allowed to slow down the exciting momentum built up at the beginning, however punctuated by citations, summings-up, transitions, or an occasional *tirade* in Ciceronian vein. The light touch only partially conceals an earnestness of purpose that breaks forth now and then with stunning eloquence. The argument lies coiled and waiting to spring, so that diversionary tactics serve to mark time until it can be stated, or restated, with full force.

The character of the "good Father" who appears in several of the earlier letters has been called by some the first truly comic figure in seventeenth-century French literature. Is he perhaps descended directly from Galileo's "Simplicius"? That is entirely possible. Stubbornly parroting the maxims of his Society he lets himself be lured into one semantic or logical trap after another, quite unaware of the noose tightening around his throat. Obviously a kind of "fall guy" in Pascal's imaginary dialogue, *le bon Père* is the liveliest of puppets who seems to be right out of Molière. He answers his questioner eagerly by citing maxims and examples, taking the bait artfully offered, until he contradicts himself, condemns his own views, or collapses into limp irrelevance. The more he praises the "marvelous" principles and "grand" maxims of the Society of Jesus, the more his words have the effect of ironic denunciation.

Indeed, the turn in the first group of letters from a defensive to an offensive standpoint is accompanied by a heightened use of irony. The Jesuits quickly retorted that Montalte (Pascal's pseudonym) had profaned holy things by ridiculing them. Even Port-Royal urged Pascal to give up his mockery. But Pascal, stung by attacks on his piety and veracity, could not stop. Scarcely two weeks elapsed between the tenth and the eleventh Letters; meanwhile Pascal changed his style, redoubled his efforts, and addressed the Jesuits directly though still anonymously.

The last eight letters drop the device of dialogue altogether
and engage the enemy on his own ground. A leaner, crisper
style is used. The *style coupé* of the later *Provinciales,* by its
very curtness, conveys a deep emotional tone. Innuendo gives
way to outright indignation. The writing grows vehement, impassioned, bitter; all pleasantries aside, a harsh and wrathful
quality is maintained.

This change in style may be due to the fact that the miracle
of the Holy Thorn had taken place, giving Pascal the utter
confidence that God was on the side of Port-Royal. What had
before been a matter of faith now became a matter of fact. The
physicians who examined his niece pronounced her cure as
without any natural explanation. Only the Jesuits refused to
believe that God had acted miraculously. Pascal, once his scientific skepticism had been vanquished, saw the miracle not
only as a sign of divine favor toward his family but also as a
vindication of Port-Royal's cause in heaven. Therefore he re-
entered the controversy more than ever bent upon exposing
Jesuit calumny and perfidy, as he saw them.

Each of the last letters begins by announcing its subject and
then proceeds to deal with it gravely and precisely. Every
charge of willful falsification or heretical arrogance is answered
squarely. The writer keeps his private emotions under control;
his letters do not breathe an air of touchy self-righteousness
any more than of aggrieved self-pity, for he knows that both
he and his adversaries are responsible to the truth. Thus the
letters are marked by a density of style, an argumentative impact, which are more suggestive of *géométrie* than of *finesse.*

In the eleventh Letter, for example, Pascal replies to the
accusation that he is lacking in Christian charity. He cites the
use of mockery by the prophets and Jesus himself, as well as by
such doctors of the church as Tertullian, Jerome, Bernard of
Clairvaux, and others. Then he repeats four rules given by
Augustine showing that "it is the proper privilege of truth to
laugh." The first rule is to speak nothing but the truth, the
second is to speak with discretion, the third is to employ ridicule only against error, and the fourth is this:

In short, Fathers, to sum up these rules, I shall tell you only this one, which is the essence and end of all the rest. It is that the spirit of charity leads us to have in the heart a desire for the salvation of those against whom we are speaking, and to address our prayers to God at the same time we address our reproaches to men.[65]

The remainder of the letter argues that Pascal's critics are really guilty of the uncharitableness, not to mention the frivolity and blasphemy, which they wrongly attribute to him; he therefore not only refutes but reverses their charges.

The Jesuit policy of "attracting all and repelling none," as Pascal labels it, is often placed in opposition to the teachings of Scripture and Christian tradition. One such antithesis comes at the conclusion of the twelfth Letter which has been occupied with Jesuit laxity regarding almsgiving, simony (buying and selling sacred things or offices), and bankruptcy. Now, turning abruptly from such matters, Pascal takes a different tack in this passage:

You suppose that you have power and impunity, but I believe that I have truth and innocence. It is a strange and tiresome war in which violence tries to oppress the truth. All the efforts of violence are unable to weaken the truth and can only serve to raise it up again. All the radiance of truth cannot put a stop to violence and only enrages it the more. When force fights force, the strongest destroys the earth; when argument is opposed to argument, the genuine and convincing confounds and scatters what is only hollow and lying; but violence and truth cannot avail against each other.

But no one should presume to think that these antagonistic forces are equal, writes Pascal,

because there is this vast difference, that violence in its course is limited by the order of God, which overrules its effects to the glory of the truth which it attacks; whereas truth lasts forever, and triumphs at the end over its enemies, since truth is eternal and almighty as is God himself.[66]

The contrast between might and right has never been stated more compellingly. Pascal's antithesis between *violence* and *vérité* has the character of a controlled inspiration, a fusion of logic with rhetoric whereby both reach their climax simultaneously and by harmonious means. Many other similar examples occur especially throughout the later *Provinciales*.

It was the artistry of Pascal's *Letters* that ensured their success. As Nicole wrote in his preface to the Latin translation, they were read by the learned and the ignorant alike and produced the effect their author had intended. Bossuet admired their "elegance," and Racine studied them for their lessons in style. Molière found in them suggestions for his dramatic writing. By the end of the century, when the Jesuit-Jansenist controversy had temporarily died down, Charles Perrault could say of the *Provincial Letters:* "Everything is there—purity of language, nobility of thought, solidity in reasoning, finesse in raillery, and throughout an *agrément* not to be found anywhere else." [67]

Written in the heat of conflict, under the worst possible conditions, Pascal's work nevertheless secured his fame to posterity. It is not to be denied that he sometimes treated his adversaries unfairly; but the same criticism can be leveled against Dante, Milton, Swift, or Voltaire. What satirist or debater is ever altogether fair to his opponents? And yet one cannot help wondering if Pascal's robust sense of humor did not more than once get under the guard of the Jesuits and make them smile at themselves. At all events, the *Provinciales* succeeded in making an artist out of a scientist, thus adding a further dimension to Pascal's "astounding genius"; and they not only prepared the way but actually prefigured his achievement in the *Pensées*.

III

The Pensées

Whereas the *Provincial Letters* met with instant acclaim, despite the fact that they were soon placed on the Index and publicly burned, the *Pensées* had a very different fate. The taste of readers in the age of Louis XIV was quite unprepared to approve a work so fragmentary and unfinished, so intimately personal in tone, and so enigmatic in construction. It was not until the nineteenth century, after various editors had attempted to restore the original text, that the *Pensées* were read with general approval. Then the very qualities that had alienated readers in earlier generations were appreciated and admired. Sainte-Beuve spoke for many others when he remarked that Pascal, whose finished writing was praiseworthy enough, was still more excellent a writer in the work broken off by his death.

Today, thanks to the labors of a corps of scholars headed by Louis Lafuma, we know that Pascal's papers were not left by him in as confused a state as was formerly supposed. Evidently he wrote out his notes for the Apology on large sheets, as he did for other writing projects, the topics separated by horizontal lines. He had begun to classify these notes himself by cutting them from the sheets and regrouping them into sewn bundles, or *liasses*, each of which was given a title such as "Misery," "Grandeur," "The Sovereign Good," or "Christian Morality." More than four hundred of the *pensées* were thus collected into twenty-seven bundles. The rest, over five hundred, remained unclassified. After Pascal's death his family had a legible copy made and entrusted it to an editorial committee at Port-Royal for eventual publication. The bundled notes were transcribed just as Pascal had arranged them; the remaining miscellaneous notes were copied in the order, or disorder, in which they were left, a few on large sheets, most on smaller pieces of the original sheets.

Strangely enough this document, the *Première Copie,* antedates by half a century the bound volume containing the original drafts of the *pensées* which Pascal's nephew Louis Périer presented to the library of Saint-Germain-des-Prés in 1711. The volume, called the *Recueil Original,* consists of large pages of heavy paper onto which Pascal's notes were pasted, their margins cut away, tucked into every possible space on the large sheets, and therefore giving the appearance of having been written on paper of different sizes and shapes. Hence the *Copie* is a more trustworthy guide to the plan Pascal intended to follow in his Apology than is the *Recueil* in its piecemeal confusion.[68]

Study of the copy is recommended by Pascalian scholars as a corrective to the overly systematic classification proposed in the first Port-Royal edition (1670). As Jean Mesnard says:

> We find a cunning interweaving of themes, a subtle, almost musical mode of composition, and an athletic and balanced mode of argument, though always a rigorously logical one. . . . We can now understand what Pascal meant, in his remarks on the theory of literary composition, by "the order of the heart," the order of emotional persuasion, "which consists chiefly of digressing on each point that is connected with the general purpose, so as to keep that purpose always in view." [69]

Yet it is the original manuscript, of course, that furnished necessary clues as to Pascal's method of writing. When he strikes out one word or phrase and substitutes another, he invariably aims at greater clarity by way of liveliness and concreteness. He wrestles an awkward sentence into simpler shape by changing plural into singular, passive into active verb, or rearranging word order. He makes repeated efforts to secure stringency and compression, as in the celebrated *pensée* on the two infinities where after a number of false starts fifteen lines are reduced to three. His preference for everyday, conversational speech makes precision difficult; but he is more concerned for accuracy than supposed good taste or purity of expression. "Nothing left out, nothing superfluous"—this was his working principle as reported by his sister Gilberte.

One of the most interesting *pensées* from the stylistic viewpoint is his description of the frightened philosopher. (E 81; P 44.) The point is to show how the force of imagination can unhinge rational judgment; the picture Pascal chooses for this purpose is that of an eminent man of reason having to cross a precipice on a plank stronger and wider than needed for his safety, but so frightened by the situation that he may break out in a cold sweat. Pascal writes it down in the natural order in which words suggest themselves, not even bothering to shape his image-idea into a complete sentence. At first, to make his point more emphatic, he had described the plank as wider "than the way ordinarily required for walking" (*que la chemin qu'il occupe en marchant à son ordinaire*), but this is crossed out and the words *qu'il ne faut* are substituted. It is difficult to bring this *pensée* over into English without adding words to the text as Pascal left it. In French, however, the disturbed construction actually expresses both the point and the picture with greater emphasis. Furthermore Pascal uses the word *suer* ("sweat") which the grammatical purists of his age had denounced as one of the *mots bas* inacceptable in polite speech. The nonchalance of the *pensée* reminds one of Montaigne, but its boldness is Pascal's own.

It is possible, as some students have done, to make a list of stylistic devices employed by Pascal as he secures attention, rouses dormant feelings, underscores crucial points, and wrests consent from the astonished reader. But it is the cumulative power of these traits which gives to Pascal's art its special texture and appeal. "It is a bad sign when the glimpse of a person reminds one of his book," he wrote. His readers have discovered that in taking up his book they were drawn directly into conversation with a many-talented and "universal" man.

One general quality of the Pascalian style is indicated by the word "vision":

> Seeing is the prerogative of genius; it discerns structures, relationships, proportions, figurations where another can only line up concepts with difficulty. The genius is one who sees and makes us see. Pascal's genius was not only that of possessing exceptional eyes but of lending them to any person of good will so that he might see in his turn *la condition humaine*.[70]

The metaphor of seeing is perhaps the oldest and most widely used of all symbols for acquiring truth or knowledge. For his part, Pascal carried visual acuteness into all his work, especially his writing. To see things clearly and to bring clearness of sight to others was among the chief purposes of his life and thought. Whoever would know things as they are, he wrote, must keep at a certain distance from them:

I must do as painters do and stand back, but not too far. How far, then? Guess.

> Pictures, seen from too far away or too close; and there is only one indivisible point that is the right place. . . . Perspective determines this in the art of painting. But in truth or morality, who is to decide this? (E 983, 58; P 558, 21.)

What has often been called Pascal's sensibility, his singular gift for fusing thought and feeling in a moment of discernment, depends largely on his talent for seeing in perspectives that reveal the truth just because they do not claim to be more than finite, relative glimpses of the truth.

Pascal's writing gains its sharpness of perspective largely through the use of familiar but well-placed and therefore arresting images. Students of his style have generally agreed on this, although they have of course differed as to its importance in his total purpose as a writer. A recent thoroughgoing analysis speaks of Pascal's "conversion to the metaphor" growing out of his everyday experience as much as from his scientific or literary preoccupations.[71] For whatever reason, Pascal was able to set aside his native distrust of the power of human imagination where his own writing was concerned, as is indicated in such passages as these:

> The letter On Injustice may mention the absurdity of elder sons inheriting everything: "My friend, you were born on this side of the mountain; it is therefore just that your elder brother should take all."

> I have my own fogs and my fair days inside me; my prosperity or bad luck makes little difference.

> Mine, yours. "This is my dog," said those poor children. "That is my place in the sun." There is the beginning and the token of the usurpation of the whole earth.

> Rivers are roads that move, and carry us wherever we want to go. (E 32, 753, 112, 925; P 9, 552, 64, 717.)

Pascalian imagery is drawn from a multitude of sources, some like music or biology on the fringes of his interest, others like physics or politics closer to its center. Often the theme is stated indirectly within the image itself; seldom is a "principle" enunciated with an image appended as an illustration. An image may be merely sketched in passing: the parrot wiping its beak although it is already clean, the doctor who goes on talking for a quarter of an hour after he has said everything worth saying, the dancer thinking where he must place his feet. But Pascal can also take a fairly trite image and turn it into an unforgettable one. The famous fragment on Cleopatra's nose gives a new and stunning twist to an old, banal figure of "the face of the earth": "Cleopatra's nose—if it had been shorter, the whole face of the earth would have been changed" (E 90; P 413).[72]

Pascal's facility with images can be overstressed, of course. He does not use them with the exuberance and prodigality of Montaigne, a more "imaginative" writer than Pascal. If, as Jean Mesnard remarks, Pascal "was a poet above all through his gift for creating images," it must be remembered too that

> these images, in his case, are never used merely to adorn an abstract idea, or even to make it clearer by a concrete example; the image, in Pascal, is of one flesh with the idea, it is summoned by the idea. It is the warmth of the argument that gives birth to the vision; it is the emotion excited by the idea that begets the image.[73]

Another general feature of Pascalian style is *rhythm*. Occasionally this effect is secured by simple devices such as alliteration or assonance, but a subtler kind of verbal music is more characteristic, especially as rhythm is joined to image to produce mysterious arousals and evocations. A short essay, in straightforward prose, on dreams and reality is concluded by this haunting line: "Life is a slightly less inconstant dream" (*Car la vie est un songe un peu moins inconstant*) (E 261; P 803). A more intricate interweaving of sounds and stresses issuing in a powerful "natural" rhythm is this passage:

Ennui.—Nothing is so unbearable to man as to be altogether
at rest,
>without passions,
>>without business,
>>>without amusement,
>>>>without employment.
Then he realizes his nothingness,
>his forsakenness,
>>his insufficiency,
>>>his dependence,
>>>>his impotence,
>>>>>his emptiness.
Straightway there will arise from the depths of his soul
ennui,
>darkness,
>>sadness,
>>>chagrin,
>>>>vexation,
>>>>>despair.   (E 160; P 622.)[74]

By virtue of his talent for combining image and rhythm
Pascal is a poet *malgré lui*. However, his use of scientific methods and models in his writing is no less striking. To take one
example, in developing his thoughts on imagination and *divertissement* he begins by drawing attention to assorted facts
which call for some explanation. A hypothesis is then put forward and is demonstrated by a vivid special case, that of the
king who despite his greatly favored position must seek distraction like everybody else to escape being unhappy. So a
"principle" has been discovered, namely, that man cannot bear
to face himself, which can account for the seemingly random
sampling of facts noted at first.

When he is searching for "the reason of effects" Pascal's art
takes on a density and strictness of approach that deepen its
tone. This is even more true when the writing becomes plainly
argumentative, as it does for instance in the famous Wager or
pari. No passage in the whole of the *Pensées* is more instructive in showing how closely style is tied to content, how in-

separably a controlling image may be fused with a developing argument.

Port-Royal published the *Pari* as Chapter VII of its edition of the *Pensées*, with the title "That it is more advantageous to believe than not to believe what the Christian religion teaches." Pascal's own title was *"Infini—rien"* (E 343; P 418); he wished to prepare the way for his argument by emphasizing that God cannot be an object of man's knowledge since it is impossible for the finite to know the infinite. He draws a striking parallel between mathematical infinity and the divine infinity, but abandons this when he makes the point that reason cannot decide that God either does or does not exist; that is only possible for faith. The abstract antithesis, finite-infinite, is now personalized into we-God. This first stage may be termed a succinct justification, in brisk declarative sentences, of an agnostic attitude toward any purely rational knowledge of God.

The second stage introduces the unbeliever or *libertin* who is asked, "How do you bet?" and answers, "Why bet at all?" Pascal retorts that not to bet is actually to bet against God. Indecision is impossible; either God is or is not, there is no third alternative, for "you are embarked." The unbeliever protests, not unnaturally, "But maybe I am staking too much," to which Pascal replies that one's own self-interest requires a leap of faith, that one may rightly give up reason in order to save one's life, when a finite reality must be staked in a game where chances of loss and gain are equal and when the infinite —eternal life—is the prize. Here Pascal, having presumably dislodged his *libertin* from the notion that his right option is not to bet at all, attempts to "prove" that in deciding to live as if God exists he has nothing to lose and everything to gain, but in living as if God does not exist he has everything to lose and nothing to gain. It is that simple. In his analysis of the *Pari,* Jean Steinmann tells of a dialogue between an unbeliever and a priest named Mugnier. "You are going to be greatly cheated after your death," says the unbeliever, "if God does not exist.' The priest replies, "And you, if he does exist?" [75]

Pascal's imaginary adversary may still confess his inability to believe in God, but his reluctance is now seen to be located in his will and not his reason. As the third stage begins, Pascal makes an abrupt turn in this direction. The way to find faith, he asserts, is to imitate those who already possess it: "Take holy water, have masses said." This is how they too begin, and their faith is still a risking and choosing rather than a rationally guaranteed procedure. Pascal assures the *libertin,* "That will naturally make you inclined to believe and will calm you." But Pascal's last word is much stronger—*abêtira.* Generations of intellectuals have been shocked by it and argued over it. What did Pascal mean as he wrote it? Probably he was thinking of the instinctual, automatic level of human behavior; almost certainly he was also trying to express something of Saint Paul's belief that "God chose what is foolish in the world to shame the wise" (I Cor. 1:27), so that faith is properly docile and humble. Doubtless the best translation of this much-discussed word would be "abase" or "humble" rather than the most literal rendering "brutalize."

What we have in the *Pari* is a carefully wrought progression of thought founded on a central image, designed to engage an unbeliever on his own ground and move him toward readiness for faith. Whatever it may be worth as an argument for God, Pascal's figure of the man at the gaming table, betting for or against God, will not cease to irritate and fascinate us. Written with ironic triviality and deceptive simplicity, the *Pari* stands for the fact that whether we believe or disbelieve, "in either case we *act,* taking our life in our hands." [76]

IV

Sources and Models

Every writer is first of all a reader whose style is shaped indubitably by what he discovers and admires in the writing of others. These influences may be obvious, admitted by the author himself or detected by comparing particular texts. Or they may be less easy to trace, yet for that very reason more pervasive and controlling. Pascal's writing gives ample evidence of both sorts of influence.

The influence of one author upon another may also involve both positive appropriation and negative reaction. This ambivalence is present in Pascal's use of his most influential model, Montaigne. He studied the *Essais* at close range, reading and rereading them for at least two years, making appreciative or critical notes, and later incorporating scores of Montaigne's expressions and observations into his own writing. His indebtedness to the great Gascon essayist is both evident and profound, and it is frankly avowed. He found fault with Montaigne for his garrulousness in talking too much about himself, for his "lewd words," and even more for his unscientific notions and his indifference to religion. Nevertheless, he recognized the merits of the *style naturel* in Montaigne, consciously emulated it, and was so strongly drawn to the portrayal of human frailty and stupidity given in the *Essais* that he confessed: "It is not in Montaigne, but in myself, that I find everything I see in him." (E 758; P 689.)

Pascal's debt to Montaigne as both a source and a model is greater than his ample borrowing of examples and anecdotes would suggest. The *Essais* served as a channel for other influences as well, especially those coming from classical antiquity. The allusions to ancient authors and personages given in the *Pensées* can frequently be traced to Montaigne, although some of these references were doubtless provided by the Chevalier de Méré also. As soon as we begin to find parallels or borrowings, however, we observe Pascal's originality at work modifying or reconstructing what he found in Montaigne. One illustration, already mentioned, may suffice. The frightened philosopher is taken from Montaigne (Essays II. 12), who describes his plight in three successive settings and then substitutes himself for the philosopher. Pascal selects the most striking detail in each scene, fuses them into one, and leaves much more to the reader's imagination, because he has as usual a particular point to make. Again and again, his brusque and pithy recasting of Montaigne's leisurely, rich prose demonstrates Pascal's personal fondness for the single impression tightly conveyed, with bold and economical directness.

Does Pascal's pointed, curt style violate Montaigne's mellow, ruminating style? That is a matter of individual preference, surely. At all events Pascal gives evidence of his independence and dependence simultaneously, by adapting the material from Montaigne in such a way as to heighten the contrast between two styles that are basically dissimilar. Montaigne always has time to tell a story; Pascal does not. While the freshness of an anecdote or comment may be Montaigne's, it is Pascal's reworking that is more memorable and quotable.[77]

The influence of Montaigne upon Pascal's thought is no less important, although not so pronounced as that upon his actual writing. The long twelfth essay in the second volume of Montaigne's *Essais* is given over to a defense of a book by Raymond Sebond on "natural theology" in which Montaigne had a special interest. He likes Sebond's insistence that "we should accompany our faith with all the reason we possess." But his defense soon turns out to be an attack, as he becomes more intrigued with Sebond's awareness of the vanity and contradiction of human pretensions to know the truth. How can we know that human reason leads to valid principles or that universal laws may be discovered from the so-called laws of nature? "Can anything be imagined," he asks, "so ridiculous as this miserable and wretched creature?" Man is the prey of his own irrationality and even his philosophies and religions only emphasize this fact, albeit unintentionally. Mere appearances are taken for realities, and relativities for certainties, in every human interest or endeavor. "We have no communication with being."

Pascal, as we might expect, finds this description of the human state entirely congenial and convincing. But he is horrified by Montaigne's lack of compassion for the weaknesses he catalogs, and still more by the pessimism and skepticism regarding man which Montaigne makes no effort to avoid. This critical response, by which Montaigne provides Pascal with material for his thought and then becomes its target and victim, is best shown in the *Entretien avec M. de Saci,* a reported interview with one of Port-Royal's clerical counselors.[78]

The subject of their conversation is the Stoic moral philosophy represented by Epictetus and the skeptical position exemplified by Montaigne. Epictetus, says Pascal, is right in holding that man's chief duty is to learn and follow the will of God; but he is wrong in supposing that this can happen through will power or rational self-control alone. Montaigne, for his part, understands the impotence of man well enough, but he sees no way out and comes to rest in a destructive skepticism which his mocking motto "What do I know?" epitomizes. There is error on both sides; the truth of one is the falsity of the other; they therefore only annihilate each other, leaving a void which it is the prerogative of "the truth of the Gospel" to fill.

Our interest here is primarily in Pascal's judgment on Montaigne's skepticism. He finds it inacceptable and tempting at the same time. In the final analysis, however, it must be rejected because it implies a low and hopeless view of man. The truth of the gospel teaches that "all that is infirm belongs to human nature, but all that is powerful derives from grace." [79] Yet this power is not some alien, external force; rather, it testifies to the greatness of the human soul, made for infinity and with a kind of instinct that "raises us up." In this respect Pascal is more a humanist than Montaigne, since he *believes in* man in the light of the Christian gospel as he understands it. "There is a God, of whom men are capable . . . and a corruption in themselves which makes them unworthy of him." What is dangerous in Montaigne, therefore, is that man "should know his own wretchedness without knowing the Redeemer who can free him from it." (E 17; P 449.)

A second source and model for Pascal's literary art is, of course, the Bible. Here the influence is so pervasive and important that it can scarcely be overemphasized. A wealth of Biblical detail in the form of copious, frequent quotation (usually from memory) and through a multitude of allusions and echoes appears especially in the latter half of the classified *Pensées*. The reader of today, lacking Pascal's intimate acquaintance with Scripture, may not recognize the extent and depth of this influence. But for Pascal, the literature of the Bible provides a resource of personal reflection, a matrix of content and style in writing, "which determines the personality of the man and the originality of his work." [80]

He worked mainly with the Louvain edition reprinted in 1615, which incorporated much of the forceful, archaic language of an earlier Protestant version. He was able to compare this French translation with the ancient Latin and Greek versions that were available, in particular the Vulgate Bible which the Council of Trent (1545–1563) had decreed as the authoritative text for Roman Catholics. Before his death Pascal had begun to learn some Hebrew, making notes on a voluminous collection of rabbinical interpretations of the Jewish Scriptures titled *Pugio Fidei*, which he cites several times in the *Pensées*. In his *Abrégé*, or *Short Life of Christ*, done in 1655–1656, he tried his hand at harmonizing the differing accounts in the four Gospels, which others like Erasmus had attempted earlier.

This is not the place to discuss Pascal's view of Scripture in detail, except as it bears upon his own literary work. He believed that the Bible was "the oldest book in the world" and contained "the most authentic history." But he was not on that account a literalist; he accepted the basic distinction between literal-factual and spiritual-allegorical modes of understanding Scripture, insisting with Saint Paul and the church fathers that spiritual things should be interpreted in a spiritual way. This meant for Pascal that much of the language of the Bible is "figurative" even when it is ostensibly factual. It contains contradictions which can be reconciled, and obscurities that can be clarified, only by the "eyes of faith" that see beyond and behind them.

The mystery of Scripture is closely bound up with its unity. The thirty-nine books of the Old Testament and the twenty-seven books of the New spell out one grandly coherent story of God's way with man, Pascal thinks. What unifies that story is "Jesus Christ, whom the Old and the New Testaments envisage, the Old as its hope, the New as its pattern, and both as their center" (E 600; P 388). He puts the same truth in another way by saying that "the sole object of Scripture is charity."

Pascal is not above using Scripture as a body of proofs to convince the unbeliever—the prophecies really predict, the miracles give evidential certainty—but he is saved from what today would be termed fundamentalism by his ever-present sense of the Bible's mysterious unity. This sense informs practically every Biblical citation and allusion in Pascal.

The signature and cadence of Scriptural speech appear in passages that seem most typically Pascalian. Fundamental images of separation from God, of human emptiness that God alone can fill, of the darkness of unfaith contrasted with the light of faith, are taken from the Bible. Others, less basic but perhaps more vivid, are traceable to the same source: man as "a worm of earth," the chosen vine that gives only "sour grapes," the seed cast into good soil, "Pharisee and publican," are but a few examples. Usually in adapting material from Scripture, Pascal gives to it an emphasis and conciseness not found in the original. Even more significant are the resonances of Biblical style, especially those of antithesis, parallelism, and lyricism, that disclose Pascal's artistic faithfulness. It is not too much to say that his ideal in writing, and the means for achieving it, came to him from the Bible. Pascal's judgment on the manner of Christ's teaching is suggestive in this respect:

> Jesus Christ said great things so simply that it seems as if he had not thought about them, and so clearly that we see exactly what he thought about them. This clearness combined with such simplicity is wonderful. (E 586; P 309.)

The third major resource for Pascal's art was provided by the works of classical antiquity. Probably he was not as familiar with these writings as he would have been if he had attended a Jesuit school where Latin was taught and stress was placed on classical principles of oratory, argument, and composition. The unconventional education he received from his father makes it difficult to guess the extent of possible classical influences. Pascal, like Shakespeare, gained much of his acquaintance with the ancients at secondhand, notably through Montaigne.

We do know, however, that he studied the writings of Saint Augustine with some thoroughness. At least eight direct references in the *Pensées* bear out this impression, not to mention references in other works. One *pensée* is a translation from Saint Augustine's *Enarrations on the Psalms* (Psalm 127):

> The rivers of Babylon flow, and fall, and sweep away. O holy Zion, where all is firm and nothing falls! One must sit by these waters, not under or in them, but above, not standing upright, but sitting down, so that one remains humble by sitting, and safe by staying above. . . . Let us see whether this pleasure is firm or transitory; if it passes away, it is a river of Babylon. (E 720; P 918.)[81]

Pascal also read the treatise *On Christian Doctrine* by the great African bishop, in which he drew upon his own experience as a teacher of rhetoric and quoted Cicero's description of the orator's aim as "to instruct, to delight, and to move." Emphasizing the need for a variety of styles, Augustine shows that the Christian teacher, although rightly more concerned with wisdom than with eloquence, must appeal to the emotions if he is ever to "subdue" them. By way of example he discusses the structure of sentences and the kinds of images that can stir the mind and sway the will.

Pascal must have responded positively to these rules for the art of persuading, since they were much like his own. Surely he was not insensitive to the actual flow and flavor of Augustine's eloquence itself; for Pascal too had his flights of oratory, being not altogether unaffected by the baroque fondness for spacious, majestic sonorities punctuated by moments of terse impact. He once summed up the Augustinian purpose in writing as "to warm, and not to instruct"; he further compared it with the styles of Montaigne and Descartes—to their disadvantage, of course.

Also there are noticeable similarities in Augustine and Pascal as writers. They shared a precious talent for intimate address shaped by the rhythms and themes of Biblical speech. In them both, an intensely moral earnestness was joined to the nuances of a sophisticated intelligence, so that the evangelist's passion kept close company with the critic's judgment. And both men were concerned that faithful witness to the gospel should find its voice as humanly liberating truth.

V

Style and the Man

Each of these models and sources must be considered indispensable to Pascal's artistic achievement, although they do not explain it fully. The secret of the style is that of the man himself. But the task of peeling back the style to disclose the secret of the man is difficult; in the nature of the case there can be no finished picture of le vrai Pascal, and the work of interpretation will go on. A "universal man" answers to many interests and provokes many more. Thus the Romantic enthusiasm for the *Pensées* in the nineteenth century produced a view of their author as a man divided against himself, hurling himself from one preoccupation to another, assailed by doubts and torn by anguish, given to excess in all directions, wasting his energies by turns in science, worldliness, and religious zeal. This picture bears all too plainly the signature of Romantic instability itself; yet it is far from having lost its force, as when serious students still claim that Pascal was "incapable of moderation," "steeped in impatience," "violent and irrational," and the like.

A strong reaction is currently gaining ground in Pascalian studies, which prefer to present him in his historical context as a man of property and business, a socially conditioned thinker, an inventor of techniques, or a strategist in communication. All this clearly reflects the dominant interests of contemporary life, and it is bracing to learn that Pascal fits into these interests. So one pores over leases and bills of sale, examines the watermarks of the paper on which Pascal wrote, or does word counts and syntax analysis, once again with the intention of uncovering the kind of man he really was. However, what is obviously missing in these un-Pascalian efforts is the style of the man himself.

"Not the writer, but the man"—thus Alexandre Vinet titles one of his best chapters on Pascal. But the writer and the man are basically the same. One sign of the human style in Pascal's work is suggested by the word "equilibrium." In his own words:

> I do not admire the excess of a virtue, such as valor, unless I see at the same time the excess of the opposite virtue, as in Epaminondas who was both extremely brave and extremely kind. . . . One does not show his greatness by going to one extreme, but by touching both at once and occupying all the space between them. (E 229; P 681.)

Since man's nature consists in movement, equilibrium does not mean simply standing one's ground and reaching out from a fixed point. Pascal even allows that it may actually be no more than "a sudden movement of the soul from one to the other of these extremes" that gives the illusion of keeping one's balance between opposing pressures; yet this "indicates at least the soul's agility, if not its scope."

These words may fairly be applied to the man who wrote them: a personality highly complex, open to diverse solicitations, prone to hyperbole and absolute judgments, but achieving nevertheless a precise if precarious equilibrium between contrasting interests and abilities. Jean Mesnard says rightly:

> We cannot radically oppose the scientist to the man of the world, or the scientist or the man of the world to the Christian; Pascal was always, in various fashions, a scientist, a man of the world, *and* a Christian. It is futile to try to set the doctrine of the *Provinciales* against that of the *Pensées,* or to try to set the dying Pascal against the living Pascal.[82]

The genius of Pascal expressed in his writing indicates *both* agility and scope, a counterpoise sustained not without self-discipline and suffering.

Another word for equilibrium is health. How healthy could a man be who, if his sister's memory is to be trusted, had not spent one day without physical discomfort for the last twenty years of his life? And yet of all the celebrated invalids in literary history Pascal stands almost alone in the degree to which he refused to let his ailments influence his work. A respected historian of French letters speaks of the *Pensées* as an antidote to be used against the "sick" qualities of modern Western thinking, raising again indirectly the subject of Pascal's humanism:

> Against this humanism of the shopkeepers, against a teaching which sees in the successes of power or money the sign of divine blessing, which confuses right with fact, which denies the tragic character of the human condition, the book of the *Pensées* is one of the most effective weapons there can be. There one discovers the same tart vigor that gives greatness to the *Provinciales*, the same refusal of facile evidence and complacent morals, the same toughness, the same healthy-mindedness.[83]

A further human trait expressed in Pascal's literary legacy is *honnêteté*—a word with a spectrum of meanings ranging all the way from honesty through propriety to courtesy. Pascal wanted to write simply as one human being talking good sense to another, whether his subject was miracles, the vacuum, justice, or grace. He realized that continual eloquence is boring, and that when his words seemed merely ravishing or delightful their point had been missed. "This firm and bare simplicity," as Sainte-Beuve termed the *honnête* quality in Pascal's writing, is an artistic achievement, an adroit use of many tones and levels of communication, but always an ardent engagement in the task at hand, the definite problem to be solved, or the particular kind of person to be reached.

And finally, the characteristic *reserve* of Pascal should be noted. He is unwilling to say more than he knows or believes in; it is as if he understands, and wants it to be understood, that truth cannot be grasped in its entirety without shattering the defensive fabric of man's personal and social existence. Not enough has been written on the reticence of Pascal, which is but another name for his compassion. He is lured and yet also constrained by the mystery of being that infinitely transcends humanity, a mystery that when all is said and done makes silence more appropriate than speech. But since this mystery also appears within the human, Pascal like any truly great artist labors to arouse and evoke it. As his older sister and his nephew claimed, his means accord remarkably with his end.

6. The Philosopher

This is not the country of truth;
she wanders unknown among men.
Pascal

Most educated people, if asked who Pascal was, would probably answer that he was a philosopher. Taking the word in its
broadest and oldest sense as the love of wisdom, they would
be right. No other term would seem to convey more properly
his wide-ranging search for intelligibility, his impassioned engagement with truth. Why is it, then, that philosophers
themselves have generally hesitated to admit Pascal to their
company? They cite the individual, unsystematic nature of his
thinking, his disrespectful treatment of perennial problems,
and his zeal to persuade and convert rather than simply to
understand.[84]

I

It is true that whenever Pascal mentions philosophers or
philosophy directly he gives an impression of disapproval, if
not high-handedness. What are we to make, for instance, of the
withering remark that all of philosophy is not worth an hour's
trouble? In all fairness it should be noted that the *pensée* in
which it occurs was struck out in the original manuscript; but
since the sentence has occasioned so much adverse comment it
may be worth the trouble of a paragraph or two.

The whole rejected fragment, one of six in the *Pensées* referring to Descartes, is this:

Descartes. In general, one must say, "That is constituted by figure and motion," because it is true; but then to say what these are and to make up a mechanistic model (*composer la machine*) is ridiculous, for it is useless, uncertain, and difficult. Even if that were true, we do not think that all of philosophy would be worth an hour's trouble. (E 174; P 84.)

Here the obvious point is that philosophy which is reduced to a single model is not worth the labor such a reduction costs. The term included what we would call today the theoretical portions of physics and chemistry as well as cosmology, astronomy, and anatomy. This usage, followed by both Descartes and Pascal, persisted until the nineteenth century in what was called "natural philosophy." Pascal, however, was more Baconian than Cartesian in stressing the important differences between controlled experimentation, on the one hand, and hypothetical generalization, on the other. He knew too much about machines, having invented one and perfected others, ever to become a philosophical mechanist. It was his competence and caution as a scientist, rather than a merely temperamental disagreement, which prevented him from following Descartes's mechanism in philosophy.

Far from being a sweeping dismissal of all philosophy, therefore, Pascal's remark—for which, it will be remembered, he did not choose to be remembered—brings into significant focus what he thought a truly philosophical orientation should provide. Here, like Socrates and Plato long before, Pascal affirms by implication the essentially *humane* office of philosophy. To him it is humanly meaningful that two and two make four, that surfaces do not generate solids, that chance can be made in part predictable and bearable. It is man who explains the machine, not the machine that explains man. A human being is matter-in-motion just as a stone or a star; but this does not define his "heart." Philosophers ought to find ways of explaining how man can be finite and yet made for infinity. As for Pascal, according to Jacques Chevalier, he may be considered a great philosopher because he concerned himself above all with the questions which a man puts to himself when he is face to face with death.

The issue underlying Pascal's criticism is so central to his own thought, and to the thesis of this book about it, that some further discussion is required. Descartes, as Pascal understands him, is committed to a single method developed from a single *point de départ:* Man *is* because he *thinks,* and thinking rightly is a process of logical deduction using "innate ideas" to arrive at "clear and distinct ideas" which in themselves assure one's progress toward ultimate or absolute truth. Pascal, however, objects that the self-intuited "I" of the Cartesian axiom "I think, therefore I am" is the wrong place to begin, since the self which Descartes wants to make the foundation of all reasoning is actually a mystery to itself, not a self-sufficient entity capable of explaining itself and all reality as well. Hence Pascal is convinced that Descartes's philosophy, wrong in its starting point, cannot provide the security or progress in thinking which he claims for it.

Pascal too begins with man thinking, but does not share Descartes's confidence in the power of deductive reasoning to control, retain, and organize whatever thoughts come into our minds. Logic, for Pascal, represents but one of several avenues to the truth. It is not on that account to be despised; but it is misused, Pascal believes, when it is made the sole, sufficient method for obtaining truth. Moreover, it lacks the pliable and persuasive quality, in short the *finesse,* needed to get at the most vital matters awaiting human decision here and now. Therefore no one model will do, since all human minds do not think in the same way and there is more than one approved path to certainty of knowledge and of truth.

Pascal's objections to Cartesian thought reflect, of course, what must have been a complicated and somewhat troubled relationship between the two men. Respect for an older and more distinguished contemporary and admiration for his mathematical and scientific achievements were clearly qualified by the familiar eagerness of a younger thinker to discover weaknesses in the work of a senior teacher. No table of agreements and disagreements can possibly do justice to this very human relationship. Not only does the fugitive and unfinished character of Pascal's references to Descartes make judgment difficult, but the absence of any record of their conversations greatly tangles and beclouds the problem. The extent of Descartes's real influence upon Pascal, and the specific thrust of Pascal's objection to his work, will probably remain open to discussion indefinitely. Nevertheless the influence must have been considerable, particularly when seen in historical perspective; for both men believed in principle that philosophy should offer practical guidance in the business of life, both came to reject skepticism as untenable, and both reacted strongly against traditionalism in the sciences. It is plausible, at least, to suppose that some or all of these ideas reached Pascal through the example and teaching of Descartes.[85]

To be sure, Pascal seems more anxious to highlight the weaknesses in Cartesianism than in describing it fairly and comprehensively. By attempting to generate a metaphysics out of a method, Descartes does violence not only to philosophy but also to Christianity. This is the point of the famous criticism of Descartes (*Pensées*, No. 1001, *Oeuvres Complètes*, p. 640), for introducing God merely to give a "little push" in order to get the world started, after which Descartes has no further use for God. This is hardly fair since Descartes "uses" God in several other ways more essential to his philosophical system; but Pascal regards this *Dieu des philosophes et des savants* as no real God at all, and so criticizes Descartes. Most philosophers would probably agree that Descartes claimed too much for human reason and would not admit its actual illusions and perversions. Pascal went farther, asserting that such philosophy is useless because it offers nothing to man at the point of his deepest need and highest hope, and that it is uncertain because it speaks too confidently of matters that are only hypothetical to reason.

Another fragmentary reference, this time to philosophy in general, occurs in a *pensée* cited in the previous chapter:

> True eloquence makes light of eloquence, just as true morality makes light of morality. That is to say, the morality of judgment makes light of the morality of intelligence which has no rules.

He explains further:

> For judgment is that to which sentiment belongs, as the sciences belong to the intelligence. Finesse is the function of judgment, geometry that of the intelligence.

Then he adds this:

> To make light of philosophy is to philosophize truly. (*Se moquer de la philosophie c'est vraiment philosopher.*) (E 911; P 513.)

On the surface, what Pascal is saying here is that genuine eloquence, morality, or philosophy can be successfully pursued without obeying formal rules. But his lightness of touch only partly conceals the serious point he has to make. A philosopher is a man and not a thinking machine. One who became so wrapped up in his own philosophy that he was indistinguishable from it would be abandoning his humanity. Therefore he should take his work, important as it is, with something less than self-importance.

Pascal makes a distinction here between intelligence and judgment, believing that both are indispensable in philosophy. He thinks of intelligence, evidently, in very modern terms as problem-solving, operational, and methodical. Judgment, on the other hand, keeps its distance from the work being done, trying to see it as part of a never-ending, larger search for truth, and asking where the work of intelligence is leading and what it is worth. To separate judgment from intelligence, out of presumed commitment to one or the other, is to vitiate both. Finesse in judging cannot compensate for lack of intelligent procedures, but an intelligence that does not understand its aims and motives is something less than intelligent. Since to think is to be human, then let the thinker be the judge and ruler of his thought.

One may also detect in this *pensée* an echo of Etienne Pascal's maxim that the pupil should be above his work. The son had learned that lesson well, as his refusal to be confined within a single vocation shows. Having the means to become a kind of professional amateur, he could practice his belief that no one occupation—or preoccupation—can exhaust a person's abilities and accomplishments. The example of Pascal's life and thought encourages one to ask just what excellence in any craft or discipline involves. Perhaps, in the kind of virtuosity in which technique can be taken for granted without intruding itself. This is so with the philosopher, Pascal thinks. Should he not go blithely about his work in the assurance that wisdom will not die with him? Like the "free spirit" whom Friedrich Nietzsche lavishly admired and tried to emulate, the philosopher will go on making his proposals about the nature of reality while entertaining a thought "in the back of his head," which looks on quizzically and self-critically. It may be that Pascal's chief criticism of Descartes was the suspicion that he took himself too seriously. At all events, he seems to believe that philosophers should not do this, as he writes:

> We only imagine Plato and Aristotle in grand academic robes, yet they were honest men laughing with their friends like anybody else. When they wrote their *Laws* and *Politics* they did it for enjoyment. That was the least philosophical and serious part of their lives. The most philosophical was that of living simply and quietly. (E 196; P 533.)

II

If to philosophize truly is to make light of philosophy, then Pascal eminently qualifies as a philosopher. There must, however, be better qualifications than this. In favor of Pascal, let us advance first of all what Ernest Mortimer terms his realism. The word in this case refers to a temper of mind that is active and outgoing, exploring first and explaining afterward. As Mortimer says, "When Pascal studied any object he was concerned with that object, not with Pascal studying it," [86] which means that for him "thinking" consisted in a series of explorations beyond himself, many of which were rewarded by discoveries. We have already noticed the visual quality so prominent in Pascal's thinking; probably *choses* ("things") is the most overworked word in his vocabulary; to know something is in some sense to perceive it; and to think well is to see things clearly. Whatever he thought about he made his own by a process that seems almost metabolic, yet this involved no lessening of distance, of judgment, of perspective. His mind was formed by what it studied. In the words of Romano Guardini,

> The objects which he contemplated, the problems which he investigated, the way in which he formed his questions, the results that he obtained, were such that they were borne by, and in turn determined, personal conviction.[87]

Hence his realistic temper keeps Pascal from supposing that he, or any thinking person, can reach a vantage point "outside" reality. He emphasizes that "man is related to all that he knows"; to him, objectivity is not to be equated with neutrality or noninvolvement. Although a maker of propositions, Pascal does not wish to be taken for one. If he had ever developed an explicit theory of knowledge, it would have been based upon two principles: first, that there is a *rapport* between the mind and its objects of which conscious knowledge is the recognition and refinement; and second, that there is a *tension* between the act of thought and what is thought about, which forbids any assimilation or reduction of the one to the other.

This middle zone between identity and difference, but embracing elements of both, was where Pascal's thought moved most freely and productively. He could not share Descartes's "certainty," the intuition of himself and his thoughts, from which the external world is to be inferred. On the contrary, Pascal took the view that while reality must include the thinking self, the thinking self does not and cannot include reality. Thus system-building in the grand manner was utterly repugnant to him, despite the fact that he could handle formu-

las and equations as expertly as any of his scientific peers. A
regard for the specific, which amounted to a kind of passion,
kept his thought constantly in motion back and forth from
facts to their interpretation, whether he was constructing a
geometrical proof or describing the "disproportion" of man
within the universe. Whenever he ventured a definition he
would mentally substitute for it the "thing" defined. Abstraction was a process he understood and followed, but his mind
remained anchored to the concrete, even when he was attempting to comprehend reality as a whole.

Alongside his realism, a further quality of Pascal's mind at
work is his persistent search for lucidity. We have noticed
this earlier on the artistic plane; but what does an *intellectual*
lucidity involve? It does not seem to be a property of language
as such, though vocabulary, grammar, and syntax are indispensable for expressing it. Nor is it the property of ideas alone,
except in the negative sense that when we call somebody's
thinking muddled or confused we must at least be entertaining the possibility of its opposite. Obviously, Descartes would
not have agreed, as he judged it entirely possible to define
exactly what an idea is and what makes it clear and distinct.
Pascal is not of this opinion. "There are *different* roads to
certainty," he stresses in *L'Esprit Géométrique* and elsewhere,
but rational self-enclosure, logical circularity, is not one of
them. No, intellectual lucidity or clarity is chiefly a property
of communication between thinking persons. It is, one might
say, an invasion of privacy by the truth. A statement or a
thought is lucid when someone has made it understandable
to someone else—not necessarily acceptable or convincing, to
be sure. Lucidity is interpersonal, dialogical, "transactional,"
to borrow a term from current psychotherapy. It occurs within
what we commonly call an exchange of ideas; and its condition is the opening of one mind to another, a reasoning together.

Pascalian lucidity is something that happens between himself and his reader. It is the reader, of course, who makes his
own decision, but it is Pascal who creates the possibility of

understanding and being understood. He was quite aware that writing may become a far more intimate mode of communication than speaking, as it can fashion an "I-Thou" situation which minimizes the hazards, overleaps the defenses and hesitations, and prunes the irrelevancies, that crop up in actual conversation. Here a thinker must become an artist in "placing the ball," in devising breakthroughs and moments of truth for the mind engaged with his in mutual search. But he does not leave thinking behind; instead, he thinks more carefully and energetically in presenting his thought. Intelligibility is something that happens to an idea. When Brunschvicg writes, *"Tout est sincère en Pascal, tout est intérieur,"* he has in mind not the trait of an individual but the way in which this individual enables the reader to interrogate himself and so discover his own hidden truth.[88]

There is a third habit of thinking in Pascal which bears upon the question of his philosophical credentials. He called it a *renversement continuel du pour au contre,* turning constantly from the pro to the con. Although he did not coin a new name for his method he employed it as a matter of principle, believing as he did that one's best protection against bias or narrow-mindedness was that of placing alongside one opinion or idea the opposed claim to truth. This sets up a back-and-forth movement by which one's thought can be corrected and enlarged. Pascal also compares it to an ebb-and-flow motion, and to what he calls "progress by degrees." The turning back of thought upon itself, repeated indefinitely, produces in Pascal's work a great number of seeming contradictions which are in fact deliberate. However, it is to be noted that these are never static but dynamic—moments or phases in an ongoing and indeed "open-ended" process of thinking. One illustration of *renversement* is the following:

> Thus we have shown that man is vain to value things which are by no means essential; and all these opinions are refuted. Then we showed that all these opinions are very sound, so that these vanities are well founded; ordinary people are not as vain as they

are said to be; and thus we have refuted the opinion which refuted that of the people.

But we must now refute this last proposition, showing that it is still true that people are foolish although their opinions may be sound. This is because they do not see where the real truth in their opinions lies, so that their opinions are always thoroughly false and unsound. (E 183; P 93.)

This method of reasoning back and forth is bound up with the striving for equilibrium and perspective which has been already noted:

All are mistaken, and the more dangerously since each follows his own truth. Their mistake is not in following a falsehood, but in not following another truth. (E 455; P 443.)

That is precisely the error Pascal wants to avoid, as much as is humanly possible. His method of swinging between pro and con is a balancing between extremes. Without supposing that he or any other person can arrive at absolute truth, he does not on that account rest in a partial dogmatism or a slippery relativism. He may be, as some have called him, the first *dialectical* thinker of the modern period. He has what can only be termed a philosopher's faith that whole and un-impaired truth may at least be glimpsed provided we allow part truths, mixed as they are with error, to be brought into critical and complementary relation with each other.

It is perhaps inevitable that this dialectical method should be denounced as being only the irresponsible oscillation of a singularly agitated mind. For instance, Jacques Rennes deals with "the case of Pascal" by comparing him to a circus acrobat who leaps from one trapeze without ever catching the other. Nevertheless Rennes must suppose that this flying jump succeeds occasionally, at least, for he writes:

Contradiction is Pascal's nature; he goes from one extreme to the other, from the *pour* to the *contre*, with the same liveliness and equal vigor.[89]

The fact of the matter is that Pascal is quite as interested in *rapprochement* as he is in *contrariétés*. Contradiction, he remarked, is a poor test of truth. The underlying purpose of Pascalian dialectic is to move the mind beyond mere opposition toward unity. By making philosophical virtue out of commonsense necessity, it brings reason to an impasse out of which there can be no purely rational escape.[90]

Twice in the *Pensées*, and by implication elsewhere, Pascal mentions an intriguing notion that may offer a further clue to the kind of philosopher he is. "One must have a thought in the back (of one's head) and judge everything by that." (E 181; P 91.) He does not tell us exactly what this thought is, for that would be to remove it from the back to the front where it does not belong. The phrase *pensée de derrière la tête* defies English renderings like "a hidden standpoint" or "deeper motives" which fail to capture the *jeu d'esprit* of the original. Was it inspired by Montaigne's use of "the back shop" in several of his essays? That is a likely guess. It is at all events an intriguing and perhaps important idea for Pascal.

In one passage he employs this expression to suggest a contrast of the popular mentality with that of knowledgeable individuals. Both, for instance, agree in honoring those of aristocratic birth, but the latter do so for different reasons than the former. (E 180; P 90.) In fact, Pascal has three attitudes represented here: the ordinary people whose respect is automatic; the "half-clever" (*demi-habiles*) who despise the highly born knowing that "birth is a matter of chance"; and the really clever who know this too, but choose to "go along" with the ordinary people, presumably for the sake of social tranquillity, which is the *pensée de derrière*.

Here the familiar themes of *renversement*, the *juste milieu*, and distance are given a new twist. Pascal's word "judgment" is almost, if not quite, a synonym for the *pensée de derrière*. Speaking philosophically, this expression is roughly comparable to similar efforts to define thought as not only objective but reflexive: man's thinking can make itself its object, turning in upon itself while maintaining a critical distance from itself. There is no evidence of consciousness apart from self-consciousness; the presence of the self in all its thinking is as inescapable as it is finally indescribable.

To Pascal, this is but another sign that man is made for infinity, for the reflexive processes in his thought are potentially unlimited. Reflection is always mobile and open. A further step is always necessary and possible. Like many of Pascal's profoundest insights, the *pensée de derrière* is only sketched in glancing, somewhat playful strokes, yet it is in good philosophical company nevertheless.[91]

To the interpreter of Pascal, the *pensée de derrière* serves to indicate that there is an idea of the whole, or *vision d'ensemble,* giving orientation to his thought, but without announcing itself as a synthesis achieved. It operates *de derrière* to activate a kind of counterpoint in which contrasting voices separate, then flow together, thus creating both structure and freedom for the thinker. Such integration as it succeeds in bringing about is an *act* of thought rather than a content; it differentiates and unifies at the same time, in the light of Pascal's principle that "everything is one, everything is diverse." The notes for his three discourses on the condition of the great include an especially good illustration:

King and tyrant. I too will have thoughts at the back of my head.
I will take care on every journey.
Size of establishment, respect for establishment.
The pleasure of the great is to be able to make others happy.
The proper function of wealth is to give liberally.
The proper function of each and every thing must be sought.
The proper function of power is to protect.
When force attacks hypocrisy, when a private soldier takes
the square cap of a First President, and throws it out of
the window . . . (E 918; P 797.)

III

What does the word "truth" mean for Pascal? Obviously it is a term of major importance to him, but we shall be disappointed if we expect to find it given a standard or uniform meaning. He uses the word with marked respect, very rarely to punctuate his own opinions or convictions. Since his working habits and attitudes have been shaped by science, he leans heavily toward a realistic view of truth. Any inquiry should be pursued with the intent that the ideas of the inquirer must measure up to the real situation being faced. Pascal, however, is equally drawn by the claims of intellectual consistency; if he is not a systematic thinker he is at any rate a methodical and persistent seeker after an ever larger truth. Therefore he does not make a choice between the correspondence theory of truth and the coherence theory. Any correspondence of ideas with realities, like any coherence of ideas or statements with each other, can be only partial and provisional; this is axiomatic with Pascal. Hence no human being can afford the illusion of reaching absolute certainty by means of thought. All our judgments remain under judgment by the real and the true. All knowledge in the last analysis is but the *acknowledgment* of that which is known.

If any single theory regarding truth counts more heavily than any other with Pascal, it is skepticism. He fights it in Montaigne because he recognizes its presence in himself. But what he rejects in skepticism is just its pretension to finality—denying in advance the possibility of arriving at any truth at all, suspending all judgment indefinitely, making a philosophical virtue out of firm, unyielding doubt. When Pascal writes that skepticism is true, he does not mean that it is the only truth. "All their principles are true, skeptics, Stoics, atheists, etc. . . . but their conclusions are false, as the opposed principles are also true." (E 293; P 619.) As a negative critique of all reasoning skepticism is irrefutable, for doubt is indeed a necessary element in any search for truth. Nothing can be proved that has not first been doubted. However, skepticism is wrong in trying to extend this necessary moment, to make it normative for all others, even to identify it perversely with the "truth" itself. The mind of man is too much in need of real truth ever to live permanently in the halfway house of skepticism. One must not simply prove one's proof, one must

also doubt one's doubt, for truth to have any meaning what-
soever. Pascal says:

> What amazes me most is that everyone is not amazed at his own
> weakness. . . . Nothing strengthens the case for skepticism more
> than the fact that some are not skeptics; if all were skeptics,
> skepticism would be wrong. (E 70; P 33.)

In order to be true at all, skepticism cannot be solely or universally true, for then it would have no case to make against
reason for engendering contradictions and falsifying reality.
Consider, remarks Pascal, how *obstinate* the skeptic is. Why
should he want to make an unjustified position out of a clearly
justifiable procedure?

Discussions of the meaning of truth are usually threatened
by a vague banality which Pascal is anxious to avoid. Hence
he uses the word *vérité* in different contexts, sometimes in
passing, but now and then in dead earnest. Men both seek
the truth and are afraid to find it. Truth cannot be shown
without being believed in; but unless truth is loved it cannot
be known. We ought to care more for the truth than for the
good esteem of others; but to make an idol out of truth
means to love it foolishly, not wisely. Truth is both singular
and plural; there are no part truths capable of being de-
tached from the whole of truth, and no one truth includes
all the others. The question about truth is a question about
every other question as well.

This does not amount to a formal definition of truth, to be
sure, and yet materials for such a definition are not lacking
in Pascal. He might have said, as Saint Augustine said concerning time, that he knew what truth meant only when
nobody asked him for its meaning. It is, as Kant was to declare
later, a regulative and not a constitutive idea—the farthest
back of all *pensées de derrière*. In this case one could not possibly substitute the definition for the thing defined without
making truth into a parody or mockery of itself. If we miss
in Pascal the decisive flourish, the conclusive word regarding

truth, it may at least be argued that this lack represents an openness to truth on his part which cannot be found in those philosophies which claim to have defined it.

What is most true about the truth, according to Pascal, is that it infinitely surpasses human instruments and ingenuity for obtaining it. He does not intend this to be taken as a counsel of despair, however. Error can be minimized and ignorance decreased. Reason is not doomed to repeat its old mistakes but can be trained to adjust to new and unforeseen requirements. And faith, while it should not confuse conviction with demonstrative proof, may humble and conform reason to that which lies beyond and above the rational. Therefore Pascal would have us get on with the task of discovering as much of truth as our human state will permit.

Truth, moreover, is a matter of *order* as much as of degree. What is true from one point of view is not so from another. The cause of error lies in not recognizing the order to which a particular truth belongs. Each insight into truth is tempted to exclude truths of a higher order; but truths of a lower order are not denied when seen from the perspective of a higher one. As Jean Guitton observes, this idea of truth allows Pascal to argue against himself, to become momentarily the skeptic or the atheist, entering into their perspectives from above them, as it were, without taking these parts of truth for the whole or confusing one level of truth with another.[92] Progress in the truth, according to Pascal, is not only quantitative but qualitative and requires *finesse* as well as *géométrie* for its pursuit.

The greatness of truth is measured by orders or magnitudes of reality, but still more by the fact that man is infected with untruth. The human world is not the homeland of truth, as something in man loves darkness better than light. Being a Christian, Pascal calls this sin.

Secular philosophies, especially the various forms of rationalism, are unable or unwilling to discern the depths of untruth in man's heart. Isolating human reason from the rest of man, and then relying on it exclusively, these philosophies fail to reckon with the whole truth about truth. This is the substance of Pascal's criticism. Their approach can only serve to confirm man's good opinion of himself, which is the very point Pascal wishes to bring to their attention.

Philosophers other than Pascal have been acutely conscious of the bluntness and weakness of rational operations vis-à-vis the truth, without special benefit of Christian revelation. Are not the failures of reason obvious enough in the world quite apart from any doctrine of sin that may be offered to explain them? And furthermore, should we not be warned against a more-than-rational view of truth which may in fact only be subrational? Pascal must have struggled with these questions, just as Kierkegaard did two centuries later. Both thinkers had the problem of making a confession of sin, the intellectual form of which is pride, an intrinsic part of philosophy itself. But Pascal had the greater problem, since he accepted the role of reason in determining truth more readily than did Kierkegaard. He also believed, as we have seen, in the objectivity of truth to the mind that apprehends it, whereas Kierkegaard could hold that "subjectivity is truth."

Pascal moved toward solving the problem of the limits of reason in a quite original manner. Reason's last step, he maintains, is to acknowledge that an infinity of truth lies beyond it. Nothing can be more reasonable, therefore, than this disavowal by reason of its own supposed self-sufficiency in relation to truth. This viewpoint is neither irrational nor anti-rational, since it holds that rational methods and objectives must be employed to the fullest possible extent. It leaves to reason the decision as to when it has gotten beyond its proper range and depth. It believes that reason, like man himself, is something and neither everything nor nothing. It does not destroy reason in order to make room for faith, but utilizes reason to prepare for the not unreasonable step of faith.

It is a tricky and difficult business, that of pushing reason by its own methods to the recognition of its own limits—as every student of the *Pari* must realize. Taken as it stands, the fragment on the wager (E 314; P 418) *is* an argument and deserves to be judged as such. It proceeds in three distinct and yet closely related stages: the first has to do with infinity, the second with probability, the third with practicability. In the first stage Pascal uses the example of mathematical infinity to demonstrate the possibility that something may be known to exist without knowing precisely what it is. For example, we know both the existence and nature of finite space, as we too are limited and extended in space. However, when it comes to knowing spatial infinity we know only its existence and not its nature, because we share with it only the quality of extendedness and not that of unboundedness. With reference to God, since we have neither of his attributes of infinity and nonextension, we can know neither his existence nor his nature. Here Pascal's implicit assumption is the classical one that only like can know like. A rational knowledge of God's existence and nature is impossible; and therefore those who believe in God should not be blamed for failing to give nonbelievers the sort of proof that believers never claimed to have.

This being so, the argument moves from the plane of rational knowledge to that of reasonable surmise. "Either God exists or he does not exist. . . . What is your bet?" And when Pascal uses the word "God" he means, of course, the promise of an infinite happiness after death and the need to give up self-love and its pleasures in this present life. The first is the prize, the second is the stake, according to the rules of the game now in progress. However, it is not a game that can be evaded, as there is no third possibility alongside the existence and nonexistence of God. The alternative which Pascal poses is inescapable; either God, however he is conceived and worshiped, is or is not. For Pascal this means the choice or decision between "eternal life" and "nothingness," a choice that is *involontaire* because one's self is never neutral where its interest is concerned.

The stake to be put up is slight, or even "nothing" when compared with the prize to be won; but the stake is certain, while the prize is uncertain. Pascal argues that whatever may be the number of chances for or against obtaining the prize, it will always infinitely exceed the finite value of the stake put up. This position is buttressed by a calculus of probabilities showing that it is unreasonable *not* to wager a finite stake, with a finite number of chances to lose, against even one possibility of gaining an infinite prize. When Pascal says that the gambler for God will lose nothing, even if he turns out to be mistaken, what he means is that the stake seems like nothing in comparison with the prize. There is always an element of risk in faith whether the chances of gain and loss are equal or unequal. It remains an *uncertain certitude,* like sea voyages, business enterprises, or battles; in all things we work as if tomorrow were a certainty when we cannot know that it is.

The argument enters its final stage as the nonbeliever asks, "What do you expect me to do?" Now that the reasonableness of believing (betting, choosing) has been shown, the time has come for doing so. The will to believe must be aroused directly, even brutally. Pascal would have been the first to agree with Lachelier, "If the hope of future happiness is based only on a logical possibility, then we must discard Pascal's wager." [93] He would go still farther in denying that any argument can produce faith. This particular argument, however, turning as it does from the probable to the practical, offers reason an opportunity "to submit when it decides that it ought to submit." In becoming *ad hominem* and "existential," Pascal's wager is left to the reader's own judgment and response. By bringing the matter of belief in God home to the will, Pascal has cleared the way for the reasons of the heart.[94]

IV

All this amounts to saying that Pascal is a Christian philosopher. His thought on many subjects was deeply informed and structured by adherence to the Christian faith. It is sometimes claimed that his allegiance only vitiates his thought. Friedrich Nietzsche illustrates this kind of response in his remark on Christianity—"that gruesome way of perishing, of

which Pascal is the most famous example." So as usual with
Pascal, the problem of credentials intrudes itself. Just what
does the term "Christian philosopher" mean in his case?

To answer this question it is important to recall that Pascal's
definitive conversion occurred after his working habits, distinctive attitudes, and guiding convictions had already been
formed. His view of the orders, for example, began to take
shape in his mathematical inquiries, but is then enlarged, applied, and confirmed by his social and religious experience.
After the "night of fire" in 1654 he undoubtedly discovered
in Christian faith the inspiring and unifying forces of his
thought, and read back this interpretation into what had
gone before. But one may say with equal justice that his own
prior thinking on the great standing questions of man's life
in the universe was instrumental in leading him to wager on
God. Thought and faith in Pascal's case entered into a
particular kind of partnership, in which the contours were
always shifting and being strengthened.

It should also be recognized that Pascal's use of Christian
resources was highly selective. There are many strands within
the Western cultural heritage which he either neglected or
rejected. His thinking exhibits little continuity with Scholasticism in comparison with that of Descartes. Indeed, he does not
consciously work at inherited problems but insists on seeing
them in fresh and individual perspectives. He regards Augustine as a fellow believer and an almost contemporary teacher,
except of course when he is defending his view of grace and
freedom against the modernizing interpretations of Jesuit
moralists. At the same time, he stands outside the mainstream
of Renaissance thinking about man represented for instance
by Erasmus, which could also appeal to classical and Biblical
prototypes. This is but to repeat that Pascal is a particular
kind of Christian philosopher, perhaps one of a kind, whose
faith and thought are related in a uniquely individual way.

The outlines of a fairly comprehensive philosophy of the
Christian religion are sketched out in the *Pensées*. Subjects
such as miracle and prophecy, Scriptural authority and inter-

pretation, church and papacy, nature and grace, and the relation of Christianity to Judaism and Islam are touched upon with tantalizing brevity and concise conviction. Clearly, Pascal planned to build the strongest possible intellectual case for the Christian faith by meeting squarely the sharpest criticisms that could be leveled against it. His was to have been an Apology which, if it had been finished, might be favorably compared with such works as Justin Martyr's in the second century or John Locke's *The Reasonableness of Christianity* in the seventeenth. As it stands, however, Pascal's Christian philosophy can scarcely be termed his chief intellectual accomplishment, despite its great suggestiveness and influence.

Every philosophically minded Christian must try to reconcile finality with universality in the truth of faith as he sees it. How is the claim to be made good that God acts once for all in one person and event to redeem the whole of mankind? Why must the outcome of world history depend so utterly upon what happened in Palestine many centuries ago? Pascal's treatment of the Christian claim for Christ is worth careful consideration, as this claim often strains the credulity or affronts the intelligence of non-Christian philosophers.

He lacked the opportunity and the incentive to become a thorough student of other religions. However, he had done some reading in the Koran as his references to Mohammed indicate. There are several of these, all polemical. The founder of Islam is "without authority" because he performed no miracles and was not foretold by prophets. He gained and tried to hold a worldly empire by violence, whereas Jesus Christ "took the road to failure" and "caused his followers to be slain." (E 403, 598; P 209, 321.) And the difference between the Koran and the Christian Bible is that while both contain obscurities equally "fantastic," Scripture alone contains passages of "wonderful clarity" by which the obscure passages may be understood:

> The two cases, therefore, cannot be compared. One must not confuse and equate things which are alike only in their ob-

scurities, but not in that clarity which makes us respect those obscurities. (E 412; P 218.)

Hence Pascal's principal objection to Islam is that it confuses the order of charity with that of worldly pleasure and power, without providing the clearness of insight to distinguish one from the other. He has little acquaintance with Islam as a cultural force, nor with its philosophical and mystical aspects; but on his behalf it may at least be said that he focuses upon the issue of prophetic authenticity which is crucial for Christian-Muslim understanding.

When he considers Judaism, Pascal realizes that a quite different set of intellectual issues is involved. The Jewish Scriptures belong to the Christian Bible; as Pascal puts it, "the Messiah has always been believed in." Judaism is therefore not to be identified with paganism. The God of Abraham, Isaac, and Jacob is the one true God revealed conclusively by Jesus Christ. Authority in matters of religious faith, Pascal believes, is derived from the antiquity and continuity of faith itself—his embracing term is "perpetuity"—and must be sought in those records of revelation and man's response to it which form the substance of Jewish history and prophecy.

What, then, is to be made of the fact that the Jews, having predicted Christ, repudiated him when he came? The discontinuity as well as the continuity of the two religions must be accounted for. Pascal does not explain Jewish rejection of the Messiah by saying that God blinded some and enlightened others, although he clearly believes that God intended to make a new start and a new people with the advent of Christ. Neither does Pascal charge all Jews with willful guilt in rejecting Christ, for that would not square with historical facts. The best explanation he can find is that many Jews failed to understand their own prophets, being tied to a this-worldly and narrowly political view of the Messianic kingdom; when the prophecies were fulfilled in Christ, these "carnal Jews" could not know what was happening or what God was requiring of them. (E 490; P 256.)

Christians had said this sort of thing for centuries, and Pascal's view of Judaism is traditional, not to say conventional, in most respects. He lived in an age when Jewish people were confined in ghettos and were compelled to listen to Christian sermons periodically; structures of intolerance were ingrained and general, as seen by twentieth-century standards. It is therefore all the more surprising to find Pascal declaring that he intends to show that "true Jews and true Christians have the same religion," which consists not in lineal descent, ritual or legal observance, nor in localized worship, "but only in the love of God." (E 554; P 453.) Indeed, for Pascal the crucial difference lies between the true and false adherents of both faiths, rather than between the two faiths as such. He is much impressed by the sincerity of Jewish writings in recording the people's faithlessness and God's displeasure with them. (E 553; P 452.)

To be sure, Pascal never abandons the idea that the Jewish and Christian Scriptures are related as expectation to realization, as preparatory to fulfilling modes of revelation. Yet "the sole object of Scripture is charity." Men and women are not saved merely on the basis of the categories or cultures to which they owe allegiance. "Jesus Christ never condemned without a hearing," writes Pascal with luminous brevity. (E 426; P 549.) Since no personal advantage before God is secured by belonging to one religion rather than another, each person must finally make his own choice between God or nothing in the spirit of the *Pari*.

Pascal was not among those Christian thinkers who claim that Christianity is inherently superior to all other religions. He did not regard Judaism as all law and no gospel; that possibility, he felt, is also open to Christians. Having studied rabbinical Judaism with some care, if mostly by means of commentaries and anthologies, he was fully aware that it could not be treated simply as a pre-Christian religion. His acquaintance with the Asian religions is, of course, less than negligible. Therefore he cannot be regarded as a serious student of comparative religions interested in describing their contradictions and possible convergences.

But Pascal was equally convinced that no over-simple, sterile rationalism can solve the problem of the multiplicity of religions for a Christian believer. He does not glory in the "absurdity" of the Christian faith, like Tertullian. Neither does he present it as a "paradox" in the style of Kierkegaard. His claim for Christ—not Christianity—as necessary for the world's salvation is an invitation to "come and see" whether Christ is not in fact *le centre de tout* in whom all divergences and contradictions are finally reconciled.

Hence Pascal loses none of his stature as a "universal man" in making his case for the centrality and finality of Christ. His lifelong search for truth leads him to discover a center of meaning, a *Logos,* in the mystery of Jesus. This discovery shapes his perspective and orders his priorities, so that his work becomes above all else a prayer, uniting human misery and grandeur in a single act—an act that does not circumscribe his sympathies or his talents, but opens them to all the fullness of God.

Afterword

Is it possible, or desirable, to make an estimate of Pascal's work and thought considered as a whole? Many are already available; few writers have been studied so assiduously or extensively as he. It has also been said that Pascal divides the critics by arousing preferences and prejudices rather than encouraging a calm, dispassionate appraisal of his legacy to us. That certainly appears to be the case; but at the same time his influence has been so far-reaching, so insinuating, that it makes some effort at assessment imperative as well as difficult.

From the viewpoint adopted in this book, such an estimate can and should be made. Its worth depends on the interpreter's willingness to accept and judge Pascal for what he was and did, instead of wishing he had been or done otherwise. He regarded his own intellectual and spiritual pilgrimage as a progression through three orders of human magnitude. This internal evidence must weigh heavily; so must the fact that even his accomplishments are marked by a strange incompleteness; they do not shine in their own splendor but point beyond themselves, calling for collaboration and response.

For example, there is the much-discussed matter of Pascal's "universality." We know how important such a quality seemed to him:

> No one passes in the world as an expert on verse unless he has put up the sign of poet, of mathematician, etc. . . . But universal

men want no sign and make little difference between the trade
of a poet and that of an embroiderer.

Universal men are not called poets or mathematicians, etc. But
they are all these things, and judges of them too. Only this
universal quality pleases me. (E 984; P 587.)

It can hardly be denied that Pascal was this sort of man himself. But how is this rare quality achieved, and at what cost?
Some "universal men" like Leonardo da Vinci attain it by
virtue of a many-sided competence that provokes amazed admiration through the brilliance of their inventions and in-
spirations in one field of endeavor after another. Yet there
are others like Goethe who set for themselves a high goal of
personal completeness which imparts to their work and
thought a kind of monumental catholicity.

The universal quality in Pascal assumes a different form,
however. He has the genius of a Leonardo for making many
métiers his own and reaching a measure of success in all, but
a basic sobriety or *honnêteté* keeps each tangential or visionary
impulse under firm control. And he possesses the sensibility of
a Goethe for human wholeness, but less self-consciously; no one
could mistake his kind of personality for that Olympian well-
roundedness so proudly sought and displayed by Goethe.

Pascal is universal, let us say, precisely in his incompleteness as a person. He never traveled beyond the borders of
his native land. An inveterate bachelor, he seems not to have
known the joys and agonies of sexual attachment or romantic
love. He took no part in statecraft or warfare, two of the
chief preoccupations of his century. Rightly or wrongly he
has been reproached with having no feeling for nature, with
lacking real appreciation for the arts, and with an insufficient
sense of history. The originality and permanent value of his
scientific work can be debated. Nevertheless, the transitional,
fragmentary character of his achievements lends to them a
mysterious quality of representativeness, of inwardness. If his
place in the development of modern Western culture is hard
to determine, his power to evoke fresh and lively response
would seem to be perennial.

In this respect Pascal succeeds where others whose achievements are more self-contained and epoch-making have failed. His success is measured by his extraordinary gift for enlisting fellow human beings in a common cause, for making them his *confrères* and companions in seeking and serving the truth. That work can never be finished just because it always begins anew. It both requires and elicits a completion that can only be supplied by others than Pascal. His insights are set forth in language that any honest person can understand, but they can be tested and appropriated only by means of the heart. He is a universal man, not in the sense that he says everything that needs to be said or catches up into his own person and work the full substance of what being human means, but in the more significant sense that he continues to be a force to be reckoned with and a resource to be relied on. It is a foregone conclusion that in generations to come, books will appear with titles such as *Pascal et Nous, Actualité de Pascal, Omaggio a Pascal, Pascals Bild des Menschen, Pascal's Recovery of Man's Wholeness*.

Whenever men and women undertake the task of self-awareness and self-evaluation, Pascal is likely to prove fruitful. His portrayal of the misery and grandeur of the human condition will awaken recognition, as his demonstration of its possibilities will excite resolution. He will always, in one way or another, be our contemporary.

Pascal's usefulness to us, however, goes far beyond that of a catalytic agent or Socratic gadfly. His thought itself will long be valued for taking man out of himself as well as for bringing man to himself. Possessing both density and scope, it combines geometric pattern and rigor with the precise perceptiveness of finesse. Pascal's thought, in fact, may be said to *achieve* its own incompleteness by building into itself the boundary of the really inconceivable. It stands as a witness to the infinite.

At an early stage of his development Pascal was fascinated by the problem of mathematical infinity, raised even by the simpler kinds of numbering and calculating operations. He quickly saw that infinity as a quantity, larger or smaller than

any known quantity, is a paradoxical idea; one cannot set
bounds to the boundless. It poses a problem that must be
recognized without being solved. A generation before him,
Galileo had conceived that there might be an infinite number
of whole numbers but could find no way of dealing methodi-
cally with the idea. A generation after Pascal, Leibniz's invention of the infinitesimal calculus, based on the use of
infinitely small quantities, changed the entire nature of the
problem and prepared the way for Cantor's theory of trans-
finite numbers in the nineteenth century.

To Pascal's mind the significance of the problem of mathematical infinity consists precisely in its insolvability, which
generates further problems of a philosophical and religious
kind. It is the theme of the two infinities which Pascal uses to
describe the disproportion between human finitude and the
infinity that transcends it on all sides, in all dimensions. It is
clear, however, that for Pascal this is not a barrier but an
opening, enabling factor in man's situation. Man is what he
is because of the infinite for which he is made. His self-surrender is, at the same time and by the same token, his self-
surpassing. True, the attempt to think something that thought
cannot think lands man in an impasse from which reason
alone cannot deliver him. But only rational thought is able to
accept its own limitations by saluting its mysterious powers of
self-transcendence. The submission of reason, far from being
its abdication or annulment, is its last and best achievement.

In the last decade of his life Pascal's thoughts turn increasingly toward the religious meaning of infinity. By giving it the name God, he enriches and enlarges his conception.
Here again, however, he is not concerned with a superbeing
at the outer edges of man's experience; he rejects dogmatic
finality as vigorously as he does rational hypothesizing when
it is a question of God. Transcendence, he thinks, is a matter
of experience, and experience is a matter of transcending and
of being transcended. The grandeur of the human soul, man's
greatness with God, now forms the horizon constantly present
to the thought of Pascal.

The central thrust of Pascal's life, and hence also the central clue to his thought, has to do with the answer he gave to his own question, "What is a man in the infinite?" He announced no arrival, but he found at long last a sure way of approach. His search for truth reached a fulfilling incompleteness in faith. He knew as well as any modern person that faith is always one option among others equally possible, since there is an element of risk or hazard bound up with any vote of confidence given to reality. He would remind us, however, that we are embarked and the heart must make its choice:

> As far as the choices go, you should take the trouble to search for truth, for if you die without worshipping the true principle you are lost. "But," you say, "if he had wanted me to adore him, he would have left me some signs of his will." So he did, but you neglect them. Search for them, then; it will be well worth your while. (E 334; P 158.)

Notes

1. *Pascal: Oeuvres Complètes (l'Intégrale)* (Paris: Editions du Seuil, 1963), p. 18.
2. *Ibid.*, p. 21.
3. *Ibid.*, p. 279.
4. See Ernest Mortimer, *Blaise Pascal: The Life and Work of a Realist* (Harper & Brothers, 1959), p. 92.
5. *Oeuvres Complètes*, p. 21.
6. Louis Cognet, in *Pascal et Port-Royal* (Paris: Librairie Arthème Fayard, 1962), p. 12.
7. Voltaire quoted in *Le Siècle de Louis XIV* (Paris: Classiques Garnier, 1947), Vol. II, p. 115.
8. *Oeuvres Complètes*, p. 28.
9. Chateaubriand, *Génie du Christianisme*, Part II, Book II, Ch. 6. See the English translation in Jacques Chevalier, *Pascal* (London: Sheed & Ward, Ltd., 1930), pp. 11–12.
10. Lucien Jerphagnon, *Pascal et la Souffrance* (Paris: Les Editions Ouvrières, 1956), pp. 50–58.
11. *Ibid.*, p. 58.
12. *Oeuvres Complètes*, p. 18.
13. Herbert Butterfield, *The Origins of Modern Science* (The Macmillan Company, 1951), pp. 56–70.
14. *Oeuvres Complètes*, p. 188.
15. D'Alibray, quoted in Jean Steinmann, *Pascal* (London: Burns & Oates, Ltd., 1965), p. 32.
16. *Oeuvres Complètes*, pp. 279–280.
17. Cognet, in *Pascal et Port-Royal*, p. 72.
18. Pierre Humbert, *Cet Effrayant Génie . . . l'Oeuvre Scien-*

tifique de Blaise Pascal (Paris: Editions Albin Michel, 1947), pp. 64–65.

19. One notable exception to this general rule is the school of the atomists, including Democritus and Leucippus, who developed the theory of the Void in nature.

20. Pascal, quoted in Humbert, *Cet Effrayant Génie*, pp. 70–71.

21. *Oeuvres Complètes*, p. 195.

22. *Ibid.*, p. 198.

23. See the résumé of this letter in Humbert, *Cet Effrayant Génie*, pp. 89–96, and the more critical treatment by Alexandre Koyré, "Pascal Savant," in *Blaise Pascal, l'Homme et l'Oeuvre* (Paris: Editions du Minuit, 1956), pp. 278–281.

24. *Oeuvres Complètes*, pp. 258–259.

25. Humbert, *Cet Effrayant Génie*, p. 138.

26. *Oeuvres Complètes*, p. 232.

27. Koyré, in *Blaise Pascal, l'Homme et l'Oeuvre*, pp. 268–269.

28. George A. Sarton, *A History of Science* (Harvard University Press, 1952), p. 594, n. 27.

29. *Oeuvres Complètes*, p. 94.

30. Koyré, in *Blaise Pascal, l'Homme et l'Oeuvre*, p. 261.

31. See Georges Le Roy, *Pascal, Savant et Croyant* (Paris: Presses Universitaires de France, 1963), pp. 67–70.

32. Léon Brunschvicg, *Blaise Pascal* (Paris, 1953), p. 127.

33. *Oeuvres Complètes*, p. 282.

34. J. H. Broome, *Pascal* (London: Edward Arnold Ltd., 1965), p. 5.

35. See the excellent treatment by Maurice de Gandillac, "Pascal et la silence du monde," in *Blaise Pascal, l'Homme et l'Oeuvre*, pp. 342–365.

36. Jacques Rennes, "Le cas de Pascal," in *Les Cahiers Rationalistes*, Sept.–Oct., 1956, No. 157, pp. 257–270.

37. Henri Lefebvre, "Divertissement pascalien et aliénation humaine," in *Blaise Pascal, l'Homme et l'Oeuvre*, pp. 196–203.

38. Jean Laporte, *Le Coeur et la Raison selon Pascal* (Paris: Elzevir, 1950), p. 13.

39. Lefebvre, in *Blaise Pascal, l'Homme et l'Oeuvre*, p. 203.

40. Jean Guitton discusses this Pascalian trait in his *Le Génie de Pascal* (Paris: Aubier, 1962), pp. 14–15.

41. The two quotations in this paragraph are from *Pascal: The Provincial Letters* (Penguin Books, Inc., 1967), pp. 294–295.

42. Two of the best treatments of the orders are those by Broome, *Pascal*, pp. 102–106, and Le Roy, *Pascal, Savant et Croyant,* pp. 87–91.

43. Henri Gouhier, *Blaise Pascal: Commentaires* (Paris: Vrin, 1966), pp. 187–243.

44. *Oeuvres Complètes,* p. 267 (letter of late October, 1656).

45. On the problem of grace and freedom in Pascal's thought, see the important book by Jan Miel, *Pascal and Theology* (The Johns Hopkins Press, 1969), Ch. IV especially.

46. The interpretation offered here differs sharply from that of Lucien Goldmann in *The Hidden God* (London: Routledge & Kegan Paul, Ltd., 1964). Goldmann regards the Pascalian theme of the *Dieu caché* as "the real center of the tragic vision" (p. 37), for which God exists only as a transcendent spectator or starer, without ever entering into the human world as revealer or savior. But Pascal's view is both more paradoxical and more coherent than Goldmann allows, chiefly because it represents an invitation to faith which recognizes the inevitability, though not the ultimacy, of the tragic.

47. One side of this conflict is expressed in Henri de Monthelant's play *Port-Royal,* where Soeur Françoise says to the Archbishop: "What you want is numbers, while we seek perfection. We have no use for half-Christians." The Archbishop replies: "No, it isn't numbers we are after. We only want to continue to exist."

48. *Pascal: The Provincial Letters,* p. 64.

49. *Ibid.,* p. 65.

50. Chevalier, *Pascal,* pp. 301, 304.

51. These writings are carefully analyzed in Miel, *Pascal and Theology,* Ch. IV, and in Broome, *Pascal,* pp. 88–101.

52. *Oeuvres Complètes,* pp. 311–312.

53. In the last few paragraphs of this section I have used portions of my article, "Pascal and the Theology of Port-Royal," in *Religion in Life,* Summer, 1958, pp. 427–437. Copyright © 1958 by Abingdon Press. Used by permission.

54. In this section I draw freely from my article, "Pascal and Jesus Christ: Reflections on the 'Mystère de Jésus,'" in *The Journal of Religion,* Vol. XXXV, No. 2 (April, 1955), pp. 65–73. © 1955 by The University of Chicago. All rights reserved. Used by permission.

55. See Abbé Bremond's "Pascal et l'église catholique," *La Revue Hebdomadaire,* 14 juillet 1923, pp. 171–183, and also his "Pascal et le mystère de Jésus," *Revue de France,* 15 juin 1928, pp. 673–683.

57. Léon Brunschvicg, *Le Génie de Pascal* (Paris, 1924), p. 186.

58. See F. T. H. Fletcher, *Pascal and the Mystical Tradition* (Philosophical Library, Inc., 1954), for a full and judicious account of Pascal's "mysticism."

59. Søren Kierkegaard, *Journals,* ed. and tr. by Alexander Dru (Oxford University Press, 1938), pp. 457–458.

60. Zacharie Tourneur, *Une Vie avec Blaise Pascal* (Paris, 1943), Ch. VII.

61. This is Jean-Jacques Demorest's view in *Dans Pascal: Essai en Partant de Son Style* (Paris, 1953). He holds that the seventeenth century did not regard the craft of writing highly, that Pascal was too proud to make a display of his skill and too honest to exploit it.

62. See the translation in Blaise Pascal, *Great Shorter Works of Pascal,* tr. with an introduction by Emile Cailliet and John C. Blankenagel (The Westminster Press, 1948), p. 202.

63. *Oeuvres Complètes,* p. 23.

64. Morris W. Croll, *Style, Rhetoric, and Rhythm: Essays,* ed. by J. Max Patrick and others (Princeton University Press, 1966), p. 229.

65. *Oeuvres Complètes,* p. 422; see *Pascal: The Provincial Letters,* p. 172.

66. *Ibid.,* p. 429; see *Pascal: The Provincial Letters,* pp. 191–192.

67. Charles Perrault, *Parallèle des Anciens et des Modernes* (Paris, 1693), Vol. I, p. 296.

68. The problem of reconstructing Pascal's plan for the Apology is too large and complicated to be dealt with fully here. In any case it has been greatly clarified and resolved by the researches of Louis Lafuma and Jean Mesnard. A helpful summing-up of present research is included in Patricia M. Topliss, *The Rhetoric of Pascal* (Leicester, England: Leicester University Press, 1966), pp. 152–186. See also Louis Lafuma, *Recherches Pascaliennes* (Paris, 1949) and *Controverses Pascaliennes* (Paris, 1952).

69. Jean Mesnard, *Pascal: His Life and Works,* tr. by G. S. Fraser (Philosophical Library, Inc., 1952), p. 148.

70. Hans Urs von Balthasar, "Les Yeux de Pascal," in *Pascal et Port-Royal,* p. 58.

71. This splendid volume by Michel Le Guern is titled *L'Image dans l'Oeuvre de Pascal* (Paris: Armand Colin, 1969).

72. See the comment of Patricia Topliss, *The Rhetoric of Pascal,*

p. 261, as well as the whole of Chapter IV regarding other major Pascalian images.

73. Mesnard, *Pascal: His Life and Works,* pp. 197–198.

74. Cited and rearranged by Théodule Spoerri in "Les Pensées de 'derrière la tête' de Pascal," *Blaise Pascal, l'Homme et l'Oeuvre,* p. 412.

75. Steinmann, *Pascal,* p. 320.

76. William James, *The Will to Believe, and Other Essays* (Longmans, Green, 1897), p. 30. In the foregoing discussion of the *Pari,* I have used material from my article, "Pascal's Wager Argument," in Robert Earl Cushman and Egil Grislis (eds.), *The Heritage of Christian Thought* (Harper & Row, Publishers, Inc., 1965), pp. 108–126. Copyright © 1965 by Robert Earl Cushman and Egil Grislis. Used by permission.

77. See Topliss, *The Rhetoric of Pascal,* pp. 268–272 and *passim;* also Le Guern, *L'Image dans l'Oeuvre de Pascal,* pp. 88–98, for further examples and discussion.

78. *Oeuvres Complètes,* pp. 291–297; English translation in *Great Shorter Works of Pascal,* pp. 121–133.

79. *Great Shorter Works of Pascal,* p. 131.

80. Jean Lhermet, *Pascal et la Bible* (Paris, 1931), p. 673.

81. See the exhaustive study by Philippe Sellier, *Pascal et Saint Augustin* (Paris: Armand Colin, 1970), and the detailed examination of the influence of the *Confessions* upon Pascal in Thomas More Harrington, *Vérité et Méthode dans les Pensées de Pascal* (Paris: Vrin, 1972), pp. 59–83.

82. Mesnard, *Pascal: The Man and His Works,* p. 200.

83. Antoine Adam, *Histoire de la Littérature Française au XVII-ième Siècle, l'Epoque de Pascal* (Paris: Editions Domat, 1949), p. 295.

84. See, for example, Emile Bréhier, *The History of Philosophy,* Vol. IV: *The Seventeenth Century,* tr. by Wade Baskin (The University of Chicago Press, 1966), pp. 126–138. Having begun by denying that Pascal was a philosopher, Bréhier then surprisingly gives an admirable analysis of his essential thought, drawing the inevitable contrast with Descartes and with the "geometrical method" in philosophy. Compare Frederick Coplestone, S.J., *A History of Philosophy,* Vol. IV (London: Burns, Oates & Washbourne, Ltd., 1960), pp. 153–173.

85. Broome, *Pascal,* gives a fuller statement of this relationship, especially on pp. 75–81.

86. Mortimer, *Blaise Pascal: The Life and Work of a Realist*, p. 201.

87. Romano Guardini, *Pascal and Our Time* (Herder & Herder, Inc., 1966), p. 23.

88. Léon Brunschvicg, *Blaise Pascal, Pensées et Opuscules* (Paris: Hachette, no date), p. 292.

89. Rennes, "Le cas de Pascal," in *Les Cahiers Rationalistes*, Sept.–Oct., 1956, pp. 236, 240.

90. In his book J. H. Broome has much to say about the dialectical patterns operating in Pascal's thought; but he interprets these patterns as evidence of a basically "synthesizing" mind—a view that overlooks Pascal's own strictures against systematic thinking and the highly dialogical or dramatic nature of his own, prompting the reader to do the work of synthesizing for himself.

91. Consider, e.g., Gabriel Marcel's salient distinction between "primary" and "secondary" reflection, Karl Jaspers' work on "self-transcendence" or Merleau-Ponty's "hidden law."

92. Guitton, *Le Génie de Pascal*, pp. 64–66.

93. Jules Lachelier, "Notes on Pascal's Wager," in *The Philosophy of Jules Lachelier*, tr. by E. G. Ballard (The Hague: Nijhoff, 1960), p. 108.

94. Here as in the previous chapter I have utilized my article, "Pascal's Wager Argument" in *The Heritage of Christian Thought*, pp. 119–123.

Selected Bibliography

Other significant and helpful works are mentioned in the text, but the list of books given here is only a sampling of a very large and suggestive literature on Pascal.

BACKGROUND

Adam, Antoine, *Histoire de la Littérature Française au XVIIième Siècle, l'Epoque de Pascal*. Paris: Editions Domat, 1949.
Bréhier, Emile, *The History of Philosophy*, Vol. IV: *The Seventeenth Century*, tr. by Wade Baskins. The University of Chicago Press, 1966.
Cognet, Louis, *Les Origines de la Spiritualité Française au XVIIième Siècle*. Paris: Editions de la Colombe, 1949.
Langer, William, *The Age of the Baroque*, 1610–1660. Harper & Brothers, 1952.
Lewis, W. H., *The Splendid Century*. Doubleday & Company, Inc., 1953.
Lough, John, *An Introduction to Seventeenth Century France*. Longmans, Green & Company, Inc., 1954.
Orcibal, Jean, *Les Origines de Port-Royal*, 5 volumes. Paris: Vrin, 1947–1963.

BIOGRAPHIES

Chevalier, Jacques, *Pascal*. London: Sheed & Ward, Ltd., 1930.
Mesnard, Jean, *Pascal: His Life and Works*, tr. by G. S. Fraser. Philosophical Library, Inc., 1952.

Mortimer, Ernest, *Blaise Pascal: The Life and Work of a Realist.* Harper & Brothers, 1959.

Steinmann, Jean, *Pascal.* London: Burns & Oates, Ltd., 1965.

SPECIAL STUDIES

Baudouin, Charles, *Pascal ou l'Ordre du Coeur.* Paris: Plon, 1962.

Cailliet, Emile, *The Clue to Pascal.* The Westminster Press, 1943.

Daniel-Rops, Henri, *Pascal et Nôtre Coeur.* Strasbourg-Paris: Editions F.-X. Le Roux & Cie., 1948.

Guitton, Jean, *Le Génie de Pascal.* Paris: Auhier, 1962.

Humbert, Pierre, *Cet Effrayant Génie . . . l'Oeuvre Scientifique de Blaise Pascal.* Paris: Editions Albin Michel, 1947.

Jerphagnon, Lucien, *Pascal et la Souffrance.* Paris: Les Editions Ouvrières, 1956.

Lafuma, Louis, *Récherches Pascaliennes.* Paris: Delmas, 1949.

Laporte, Jean, *Le Coeur et la Raison selon Pascal.* Paris: Elzevir, 1950.

Nedelkovitch, D., *La Pensée Philosophique Créatrice de Pascal.* Paris: Felix Alcan, 1925.

Strowski, Fortunat, *Pascal et Son Temps,* 3 volumes. Paris: Plon-Nourrit, 1921.

Vinet, Alexandre, *Etudes sur Blaise Pascal.* Paris, 1876.

Index

INDEX